Advanced
Table Tennis
Techniques

Advanced Table Tennis Techniques

How the World's Top Players Win

by Chester Barnes

with line drawings by
Sylvia Gainsford

ARCO PUBLISHING COMPANY, INC.
New York

The publishers acknowledge with gratitude the provision of photographs by *Table Tennis News* and Mr A. M. Ross.

Published by Arco Publishing Company, Inc.
219 Park Avenue South, New York, N.Y. 10003

Printed in Great Britain

Library of Congress Cataloging in Publication Data
Barnes, Chester
  Advanced table tennis techniques
1. Table tennis. I. Title
GV1005. B33   1977   796.34'6   76–52386

ISBN 0–668–04233–8
ISBN 0–668–04236–2 pbk

CONTENTS○

INTRODUCTION○

Today, table tennis is the biggest international sport in the world. More countries play it than take part in the Olympic Games or the World Cup and seventy-five countries are competing in the world championships in Birmingham (England) in 1977. There are over one and a half million registered players in the United Kingdom alone. In China, where it has become the national game, more than three hundred million play it.

Once giggling young ladies and un-athletic youths tentatively patted a little white ball across the net in a parlour game called ping-pong. Today, superfit athletes, coached and trained to a peak, their bodies subjected to special diets and intensive exercises, blast the ball towards opponents at speeds of over 100 m.p.h. and with such violence that the ball has been known to disintegrate. In Japan and China, table tennis champions are revered and rewarded as handsomely as pop stars in the West.

Today, too, rivalries are international and for some countries table tennis is a matter of national prestige. Partly as a result, the game itself has changed almost beyond recognition in the past thirty years. Now it is tough and becoming increasingly professional.

The first world championships were held in London in 1926, and a mere seven countries competed. Since then, there have been thirty-four world championships. By the early 'thirties, the English had lost their world pre-eminence (Fred Perry, the last Englishman to win the Wimbledon singles title, had won the world table tennis crown in 1928-29). Success passed to emigrants from eastern Europe and Victor Barna and Richard Bergmann became living legends, Barna alone winning sixteen world titles, doubles and singles. By the Second World War, table tennis had captured the imagination of half Europe. In particular, Hungary and Czechoslovakia were producing world-class players and new techniques.

The Hungarians, Czechs and English continued to dominate the game in the immediate post-war era. In 1949, Johnny Leach became the second Englishman to win the world title. By the early 'fifties, tournaments were drawing up to fifteen thousand people, even in Britain. Then an unlikely challenge arose. In 1952, the Japanese erupted on the international scene and the game was never the same again.

What was startling about the Japanese invasion was not only the nature of their equipment – they introduced bats made of sponge – but the way they revived the old-fashioned penhold grip dating from the days of ping-pong. For almost a decade, the agile Japanese, fierce, aggressive and immensely quick, dominated world table tennis. They revolutionised the game by their kamikaze tactics. Barna, Bergmann and Leach had towered above their fellows by virtue of superb defensive play, with a whole range of beautifully executed spins, chops, backhand smashes and the like, all themselves a by-product of the shakehand grip still in use throughout the West. This style of play was pushed aside by the sheer weight, speed and ferocity of the Japanese blitzkrieg. It was not until 1959 when the Chinese who, incredibly, proved even faster and more agile than the Japanese, emerged from behind their Bamboo Curtain, that the Nipponese hold on the game was broken. In the six years that followed the Chinese game reigned supreme.

The European tradition was only restored when the Swedes who had begun to train and coach their players with the kind of dedication normally employed only by football clubs, broke the Asian stranglehold. In 1972, eighteen-year-old Stellan Bengtsson won the world title in Japan. The Swedes, as part of their intense approach, had sent Stellan to live and play in Japan for six months beforehand. More recently, with players of the calibre of Jonyer and Klamper, the latter coached by the great Berczik, Hungary has once again begun to dominate the world game. As they adapt themselves to an increasingly professional attitude towards the game, the Europeans have become at least the match of the hitherto more dedicated Asians.

The aim of this book is to show the table tennis player who already has a fairly good knowledge of the game, how to bring himself up to advanced standards by a study not only of the latest equipment used in the top tournaments but of the new techniques and new skills demonstrated by the best players in the world today.

EQUIPMENT.

Sponge has probably done more to revolutionise the game in the past thirty years than anything else. The original table tennis bat or racquet could scarcely have been simpler. It was made of vellum – the material you find stretched on a drum. This was replaced by wood which, in turn, gave way to a plywood bat with cork facings. Then some genius discovered that he could hit much faster if he substituted rubber for cork. With the arrival of synthetic rubber we got the bat that Barna, Bergmann and Leach used; a middle of plywood, covered each side with dimple-rubber. With the dimples facing out, of course. This not only speeded up the game but allowed the best players to develop a sophisticated style full of subtleties and wide-ranging techniques. The ball could be made to spin in bewildering fashion and at top speed. Strokes such as the chop became an integral part of the technical equipment of any first-class player.

In the season 1951-52 all was changed when the Japanese turned up – or more particularly when Satoh turned up. At this time there was no really standardised table tennis racquet; a player could use anything he fancied. The same is still true in that many first-class players continue to experiment with materials such as fibreglass. But with the arrival of Satoh it became clear that there had to be limits as to what kind of bat was used for Satoh's was one of the most extraordinary ever seen in the game. It was an enormous sponge bat – it looked like an ordinary bath sponge, consisting of a middle of wood with outer facings of pure sponge, two inches thick, on each side.

It almost destroyed table tennis. Satoh was not a great player, but with that bat, he was like a 1977 Formula One Grand Prix racing car taking on a 1932 Austin Seven. No one had ever seen such speed. When he hit a ball, nobody could return it. He did not have to develop superlative skills; he simply stuck his bat out, touched the ball – and sheer blinding pace beat everyone in sight. Games became farcical. In the end, the Table Tennis Association was compelled to ban it. Bats became standardised and we had the development of the sandwich bat. In the centre there is a traditional layer of wood which is then covered with a thin layer of sponge and finally an outer cover of dimple-rubber. The result was a much faster game than had been usual before Satoh – but not so outrageous that play became impossible. In general, the addition of the thin layer of sponge gave the racquet more bounce, more speed. At the start, there were no restrictions on width – but it soon became apparent that if players' abilities were to mean anything, the bats used had to be as nearly alike as possible. To this end, it was decreed that no table tennis bat could be more than two millimetres thick on either side.

Nothing ever stands still, however, and a new bat was developed around 1970 by the French as a method of tackling the loop (described later in detail) – the shot that really dominates table tennis today. This racquet has become known as the anti-loop. It consists of a layer of *natural* rubber superimposed on the thin skin of sponge covering the plywood centre. It was developed at a time when the whole style of the game had changed. In the old days, a game of table tennis could continue for hours with those who had perfected defensive play generally coming out on top. Barna, Bergmann, Leach were all great defensive players. With the advent of sponge, however, attack and aggression became the norm and instead of long rallies, players went for a quick kill. Rallies became shorter and shorter and the technical skills involved more profound. Fitness, dedication, concentration, agility – all the attributes of a natural athlete – counted for more and more. Shots became increasingly spectacular. Players were forced to move further and further away from the table.

These stylistic developments can be seen as paralleling, to some extent, developments taking place in lawn tennis. Watch an old film of Fred Perry in action when he was winning Wimbledon; his game was essentially one of long and arduous rallies with the ball constantly hitting the baseline. Then in the post-war era, the tactics became those of the smash and grab – the big serve followed by the attack from the net.

The new reversed sandwich bat as it is called, produced an entirely new style of play which I will discuss later in detail. Good players could get more top spin on. Indeed there was more spin all round, but not at the expense of speed although it was inevitable that in a game increasingly dominated by speed, attack, aggression and spin that someone should take refuge in a slightly more defensive role. The French, therefore, came up with this outer covering of natural rubber.

The effect was at first sensational. Almost as great as with sponge. The plain natural rubber deadened or neutralised the spin already on the ball. In effect, the spin did not affect the receiver. It either caused the ball to lose pace and spin or simply returned the spin the hitter had sent over. An attacker sending over a smashing loop or producing a shot with terrific side spin would find the effect on the receiver negligible; more often than not, the attacker's own strength and skill became the weapons of his own defeat. Suddenly the relatively indifferent French were winning titles from nations which, technically at least, had been considered their superiors.

Plain natural rubber today constitutes a basic ingredient of the reversed sandwich bat. A minor development from the French bat is the use of natural rubber with a plain face on the outside and a dimpled face on the inside, next to the sponge. Some of the top players vary the facings of their bats – the front having a different facing to the rear – so that they can break up the rhythm of a game by abruptly hitting with the other side. I myself play with two millimetres of facing on the front and only one millimetre on the rear.

Today, the trick is to buy the deadest rubber available, most of it imported from Japan, which usually looks like somebody's cast-off radial tyre. You can test the effect if you lay two bats on the floor and drop a table tennis ball from a height of ten feet. With the ordinary reversed sandwich bat, a ball dropped from ten feet should bounce back at least five feet. The same ball dropped from the same height on to a natural rubber bat would almost certainly bounce less than a full inch.

One of the attractions of table tennis, of course, is that it has always been among the cheapest of games to play. Once you could buy an adequate table tennis racquet for fifty pence. With the arrival of the more sophisticated bats, however, prices have leapt and a good racquet, even allowing for inflation, is now expensive. Worse, the life of natural rubber is short. Air affects natural rubber to an extraordinary degree. When you buy it, it comes wrapped in plastic sheets but once these are taken off, the life immediately begins to go out of it. Within three months, the modern reverse bat is usually finished. However, to play the game at top level today, one has no recourse but to use it.

Most of the factors leading to the game's evolution have arisen from the efforts of players to make themselves even more adept. Recently, however, changes have been foisted on the world game by circumstances which nobody could have foreseen.

Traditionally, table tennis balls have been made of celluloid. But there is now a world shortage of celluloid and the traditional ball has been replaced by something called the Superball. There is only one word by which I can describe it – hopeless. It looks, feels and plays like a piece of plastic and simply doesn't work properly. Yet it has, incredibly, again speeded up the game. The trouble with it, however, is that it lacks true bounce. It hits the table in front of you and comes through at a terrific rate – but with the bounce all wrong. With the traditional ball, it didn't matter how hard your opponent hit, once you had adapted yourself to his game, you could always play him. With the Superball, this is no longer true. The ball, *skids* through your defence. Worse, after three or four games, this new ball gets a shine on it. Once it becomes shiny, it becomes even more difficult to play because you cannot get a grip on it with your bat. You cannot control it properly and some of the best players in the world absolutely refuse to play with it, insisting that it makes table tennis a game of chance. Instead of being able to rely on skill, the game depends on whether the ball jumps high or skids through unexpectedly. The necessary concentration, too, puts an extra strain on the skilled player who has been used to taking certain liberties knowing that he can normally judge the ball's flight to a millionth of an inch. Although one is not supposed to, top players do take their eye off the ball, relying on their developed instinct. Often this is in order to watch what your opponent is doing.

With the Superball, skill and technique have become less important. The effect has been to once again make it difficult for the defensive player. The situation for them has become absurd. When back defending, they find a ball shooting here, another bouncing off there. Their only answer is to step in and attack so that once again the emphasis has swung to the attack.

To sum up about equipment, the important recent changes have been sponge, natural rubber and the plastic ball. Bats, I repeat, have become expensive. You can pay up to £15 (about $24) or more for one due to the high cost of imported Japanese rubber. Yet it is impossible to play the game well without this kind of investment.

There are arguments, of course, about whether a bat should be square or round. The Japanese like square bats, the Chinese round. Personally I find that the square bat suits me best as it gives a greater area of blade. I have found myself "losing" balls on the curved segments at the top of round bats; balls that I would have caught quite cleanly with a square bat. I don't just consider this a psychological thing – but psychology plays an important part in the game and if you *think* a round bat suits you better than a square one, by all means hang on to your preference.

It is much the same problem with weight and thickness. I advise you to practice with different weights until you find the one that suits you best. Most clubs possess a variety of weights and thicknesses so you should try several out before deciding to go off and buy your own.

Remember that a bat can be *less* than two millimetres thick but not *more* or any one side. I know many good players – Surbek, the world ranking Number 3 and Desmond Douglas, the English international among them – who use bats no more than one millimetre thick, arguing that because their bats are lighter, they can get more control with them. While I think a lot of their argument is more in the mind than anything, I repeat that the best bat for you is the one which *suits you* best. Having found the thickness and weight that suit you best – and I emphasise that this must vary from individual to individual – I suggest you buy *two* bats. The reason for this is obvious; if you lose one, you will not find yourself in trouble trying to play with a strange bat.

Again, if you want to play top class table tennis, you need to keep replacing the rubber regularly so it is as well always to have one bat in prime condition. As the rubber on one bat loses its force, you can always switch to your second while getting new rubber for the first. I replace my rubber every four weeks. This is pretty expensive and until you are playing at international level, such an outlay may be a luxury. For the average club player, a new rubber once a season is usually enough. If you are better than average, or are hoping to prove yourself better than average, then you must be prepared to invest a bit of money in securing the right tools.

There are several different brands of rubber available. You can buy all and every type of equipment at any good sports shop. There is 'Butterfly' and – probably the most popular – 'Yasaka'. My advice again is to try out as many of these rubbers as possible until you find that best suited to you. I cannot overemphasise the importance of realising that almost everything depends on how *comfortable* a bat lies in your hand, how easy you find it to forget that you are holding it. Your best bat is the one that you are not conscious of, that has become an extension of your body like your hand.

Now here are a few do's and don'ts which I believe will not only help you to improve your game but keep you constantly playing well:

Keep your racquets clean at all times. Dirt on the reverse means that the surface will lose all its effectiveness and grip. A few drops of water and a few careful wipes with a clean piece of cloth will do the trick.

Sandpaper the shoulder of your bat before you play with it so as to avoid blisters. Some players wrap a strip of towelling round the shoulder to avoid blisters but I personally find that this interferes with my "feel" of the bat and anyway, the towelling tends to make the bat too bulky and even increases the weight in the wrong place. For me, the ideal is to get my hand as close to the bat as possible. Gentle sandpapering will help reduce the "edginess" of the shoulder. The importance of keeping the same bat as long as you can should also be obvious here: every time you change your bat, your hand has to get used to a new contour or set of contours and will inevitably lead to blisters. With the old bat, you have developed callouses in the right places.

Keep your bat or bats in plastic or canvas covers when not in use.

Keep your bat or bats out of the sun (never toss them on to the back shelf of your car, for example, leaving them to broil in a hot sun). At home, keep them away from hot stoves or central heating radiators – there is no need to go to excessive lengths like stowing your bats in a refrigerator! The important thing is to remember that the sun – or excessive heat of any kind, takes the life out of your natural rubber and shortens its span of use.

Never stick a table tennis ball inside your racquet cover with the racquet. This is bound to create small "dents" in the rubber and gradually ruin it.

So far as clothing is concerned, the rules of table tennis are flexible. They simply insist that you must wear dark-coloured clothes, never light-coloured ones. Yellow or any of the light pastel shades, therefore, are out. Shirts and shorts should be in the dark colours – dark blues, dark greens; the reason is obvious enough. A table tennis ball, being white, must show up against your opponent's body.

Shirts and shorts ought to give you no trouble; simply buy your regular size. The shirt should be short-sleeved, naturally. Shoes and socks, however, need a little extra attention. I always play in canvas shoes from Japan called 'Tiger'; these are about half the weight of comparable British-made shoes and I find that they are better for moving about and don't tire my ankles so fast. There are other super lightweight shoes and again you should try to find the weight that suits your temperament best. Of more importance, I think, are the right socks. I found that ordinary nylon socks gave my feet blisters, particularly as top players travelling all over the world have to run about on so many different kinds of floor surface. I now buy lawn tennis socks which have specially padded soles.

Physical good feeling is an essential factor when you are playing table tennis. You can win or lose a match depending on whether you are too hot or too cold, and whether you go into a game too stiff and not loosened up enough.

More and more top players equip themselves with at least two track suits – some of the top men with three – to keep their bodies at a pleasant temperature before they start a tournament. Some stadia and halls on the international circuit can be bitterly cold places so two or three suits can be a necessity. Even if you are playing in a temperate climate, you will benefit from at least one track suit. It will help to keep you pleasantly toned up before a game and is essential *after* a game to prevent chills.

Lastly, a final tip regards clothing: equip yourself with a glove. One will be enough as you only want it for your playing hand. Time after time I have found that when you're on the international circuit you're bound to find yourself playing in an icy hall. Without a glove, you can find your hand and wrist losing their sensitivity through cold and for the first twenty minutes of what might be a vital match, you are playing at a needless disadvantage.

*   *   *   *

There have been no startling changes in other table tennis equipment over the past thirty years but it is as well to know exactly what international standards are. The table must be nine feet long (2.74 metres) and five feet wide (1.52 metres) with a playing surface two feet six inches

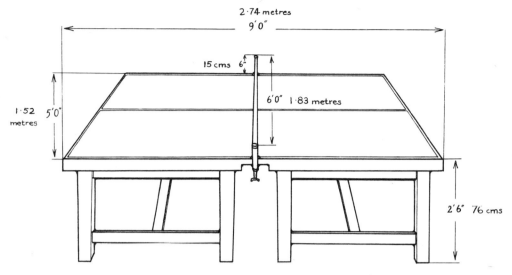

Table tennis table showing standard dimensions

(76 cms) above the floor. There are no restrictions on the composition of the table other than that it must yield a uniform bounce of not less than eight and three quarter inches (23 cms) and not more than nine and three quarter inches (25 cms) when a ball is dropped from a foot (30 cms) above it. The ideal colour is green with a matt finish and the table should have a white three quarters of an inch (2 cms) broad line painted along the edges. The lawn tennis baseline becomes *the end line* in table tennis. The term *sideline* is used in both games and in table tennis refers to the white strip lines marking the right and left edges of the table. A white centre line, one eighth of an inch (0.3 cms) broad, should be painted down the centre of the table each side of the net into two halves for doubles. This line has no significance in the singles' game.

The net, which runs across the table, parallel to the end lines, has to be six feet (1.83 metres) in length. The top of the net must be a uniform six inches (15 cms) above the playing surface along the whole of its length, with the lower edge sufficiently close to the table surface to ensure that the ball cannot pass under the net. The whole net is fixed by a cord at each end to upright posts six inches high and rising vertically six inches outside the side lines.

The ball's diameter must not be less than one and a half inches (4 cms) and should weigh not less than thirty-seven grains (2.40 grams) and not more than thirty-nine (2.53 grams). It has to be made of celluloid or a plastic material similar to it and should be finished in white matt.

TRAINING。

The Japanese were the first to start circuit and exercise training – a system now adopted by every country in the world. Basically, circuit and exercise training means that a given series of practice shots and of physical exercises are religiously worked through from beginning to end, always in an agreed order. When you get through to the end, you recommence at the beginning again, hence the use of the word 'circuit'.

All the leading countries, of course, have by now developed "training camps" both at junior and senior level. For example, in England, each region administered by the English Table Tennis Association has seven or eight training centres with proper coaches and facilities where both juniors and seniors can attend for a week or a fortnight or even longer if they wish, in order to sharpen up their games.

The intensity of training and exercise varies not only from one centre to another but from country to country, largely depending upon the seriousness with which each country takes the game as a national pursuit and the finance available. It is rumoured, for example, that the Chinese went to extraordinary lengths to prepare their players for international competition. It is said that they spent long periods chopping down trees in forests; that they attached leaden weights to their legs and arms while practising to develop muscles and speed.

Certainly at top level, training is intense and continuous in all the leading countries. The Swedes, who prepare their national squad more thoroughly than any other country in the West (at least outside the Iron Curtain) keep their team together in hotels or training centres for most of the year, generally only allowing them out to attend tournaments with odd intervals for holidays and relaxation. Not all countries, of course, are so well prepared or have the financial backing available to the Swedes. Behind the Iron Curtain, of course, the game is subsidised. One

Hungarian player was supposed to be a stationmaster but he had never even been near the station he was supposed to master. The extent and intensity of training, therefore, varies considerably from country to country. Most countries find it enough to bring their national squads together three or four weeks before an important tournament.

It is a spartan life. The English squad, for example, is expected to be up and out of its bunks not later than seven. The first exercise is a sharpish forty-minute run followed by breakfast. The appetite is always heightened by exercise so one eats a big breakfast. This is beneficial for it helps to improve stamina.

This is followed by a short lull for it is silly to start strenuous exercises too soon after eating. Then squad members repair to an indoor hall for limbering-up exercises. All traces of lingering sluggishness are quickly removed. The squad jogs, does sit-ups, press-ups, frog-leaps, touches toes, swings arms, does neck-rolls, stride jumps, hand pushes, trunk rolls and partner exercises.

Jogging consists of running around the room at a gentle trot. A sit-up is when you lie down on the floor, stretch out, then sit up and touch your toes. In a frog-leap, you simply squat down like a frog and then leap forward in a frog-like way. Press-ups and toe-touching are the exercises children are taught at school. Swinging your arms helps to loosen up your most important asset – you should throw your arms backwards and forwards and then swing them round in a complete circle. The hand push is meant to loosen your wrists and increase their suppleness. You do it by adopting a stance, then pressing one hand against the other with all your force. Both the neck roll and the trunk roll more or less explain themselves – with the former you roll your neck about, with the latter you repeat the exercise, only this time using the trunk of your body.

Partner exercises are really advanced training and should be performed only with a proper trainer in attendance. The danger is that you can easily pull a muscle or otherwise injure yourself.

Fitness is the essential weapon in your armoury. Surbek of Yugoslavia, the world's ranking Number 3 does not possess much natural ability but wins most of his games because he is extremely fit and gradually wears his opponents down. Natural flair and talent will bring you a long way but not necessarily to the top – you have to be in peak condition. All the skill in the world will not save you if you are under-par physically and your opponent is trained to his peak. I advise that you

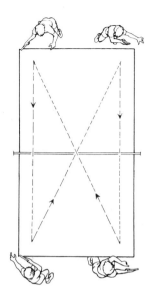

Forehand and backhand exercise

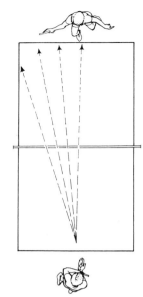

Feeding and receiving exercise

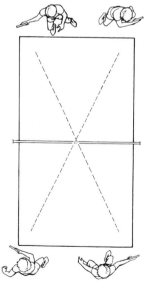

Top spin, push and chop exercise

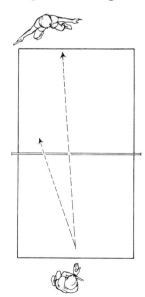

Hitting short and deep exercise

keep constantly on your toes by performing some of the exercises I have described before you take part even in a club game. Then, having reached your peak, fight to preserve it and battle continually against the deterioration process. At top level, superiority is always balanced on a very fine edge and the advanced player can leave nothing to chance.

After these limbering-up exercises, a series of playing exercises should follow. These are:

1. **The server hits the ball across the table from right to left; his opponent smacks it back straight down the line. The server hits it with his backhand, then drives it across the table from left to right and his "opponent" now drives it down his left-hand line to the "server's" forehand who then starts off the process all over again. The idea here is to start slow**ly and then increase tempo and speed but retain accuracy. Five minutes is generally enough as the "server" will have covered more ground than his opponent and the players should change over. This exercise gets your feet moving – improves and sharpens your agility – and also gives you terrific practice on both your forehand and backhand.

2. In this exercise, the server merely acts as feeder. He drives the ball down the centre-line and his opponent hits it straight back. The server then serves a little to his left and on each return, widens the angle so that his opponent, who plays every shot with his forehand, gets practice hitting from every angle where he can conceivably employ his forehand. Again, the process should be gradually speeded up. Feeder and receiver should change positions every five minutes so that both extract maximum value from the exercise.

3. This exercise is played from corner to corner and is called top spin, push and chop, (see pages 44-77). It brings your whole game into action. The server commences by hitting a forehand drive across the table. The receiver returns it with top spin. The server makes his return with a chop which the receiver returns to him with a push. Finally, the server sends it back with top spin. This exercise should be performed with both backhand and forehand.

4. In this, the server, or feed, hits the ball just hard enough to make it drop over the net, making the receiver come in; then he hits the next ball very deep, forcing the receiver to come in and out increasingly fast to unsettle him.

5. Practice spin services, along with follow-ups. (See pages 38-43.)

6. Practice the chop service which gives the receiver the chance to return a full-blooded loop drive, (see pages 59-68), which the server must block back, (see page 66). This provides excellent training in taking the loop, the big shot in modern table-tennis.

Dragutin Surbek, Yugoslavia, illustrating how to return a short service

All this is pretty strenuous stuff and at the end of each exercise, the pulse should be taken as a matter of precaution. Most people would be surprised by the tremendous increase in pulse rate.

Lunch breaks the day very pleasantly and is followed by a lie-down. Hard training recommences fairly promptly, however, although one deliberately begins with a relaxed exercise. Thus the next hour of so is likely to be spent playing football, taking on the girls in the squad at net-ball of even enjoying a soothing spell on the trampoline. An hour or so of this and its back to the table – and work. It matters little what you do during this session, as long as you are working on your weaknesses or perfecting your strengths. In general, the greater part of this period should be spent on the service – followed by real competitive work in a doubles or even a round-robin tournament.

By tea-time, you should be feeling the pace a bit, especially in the early days of training. After tea, though, it's back to work again with "free" work; that means, practising any exercises you want to, and following no set pattern.

Bed should be scheduled for nine p.m. That may seem an imposition but in fact one is generally so tired that bed is usually greeted with pleasure. This makes up a single day's pattern and you should stick to this throughout your entire period in camp. Initially one imagines that one is bound to crack up but after a day or two, the stiffness leaves you and you begin to feel in top trim.

Training camps or centres are absolutely essential to any country which takes its table tennis seriously. But table tennis is about individuals – and you cannot coach or train all individuals to exactly the same specification. What works for one doesn't work for another. Certain famous players, for instance, depend almost entirely on physical fitness. Surbek, because he relies mainly on forehand top spin and has to cover a great deal of ground during a match, never takes on a top-class opponent without being trained to his limit. The same goes for Itoh of Japan, a former world champion – the champion who had the worst backhand any world champion ever had in my opinion – who also needs to be in top condition to win. Both of these players train hard because they are aware that they can be conquered by inferior players whose style allows them to take less out of themselves during a match. Itoh, in particular, used to terrify me with the thoroughness of his preparations. I have seen him do press-ups with another man sitting on his shoulders. And again, with his legs apart, roll his head on the floor when the best most of us can do is get our fingertips down there. Such players make up for a lack of range and variety in their strokes and general play by always entering a match so fit that sheer athleticism pulls them through. For other players, the effort to remain at such a peak of physical fitness is impossible and if they tried it they would soon run themselves into the ground. In this latter category are mainly those players who possess a great deal of natural talent and a wide repertoire of strokes. Both coaching and training very much need to be tailored to each individual's own needs.

Diet is not a problem that looms large in top-level international tennis although both the Chinese and the Japanese tend to bring supplies of their own delicacies with them when playing abroad. In my experience, players from the most successful countries concentrate upon eating as much as possible. You rarely see an obese table tennis player, however; food is quickly burned up during a tournament.

So far as diet is concerned, the only general guidelines are that one should eat sensibly – avoid unusual or spicy foods which may upset your stomach – tuck away as much as you can but never eat a big meal before you go into a match. I have always made it a point of studying each round of a tournament draw beforehand to determine the time I'm likely to be at the table, and then arrange to have my meals *after* the game. The effect of a big meal before a game can be disastrous, for it can make your game lethargic.

Take plenty of salt tablets during a tournament. If possible, don't smoke and, of course, avoid alcohol. The best all-round drink for a table tennis player is milk.

Fitness is essential, but try and avoid swimming, particularly immediately before or during an important tournament where you want to catch the eye of selectors. Swimming and table tennis do not go together because one loosens up the muscles, the other tightens them.

Some of the world's top players favour embrocations similar to those used by football trainers on their charges to keep their muscles loose. Jonyer of Hungary, who took the world title in 1975 is one. He almost smothers himself in the stuff. On the other hand, none of the English national squad bothers and again this must be considered a matter of personal preference.

Three areas, important in the make-up and equipment of any good table tennis player, really lie outside any consideration of physical attributes or preparation – temperament, concentration and psychology.

There is not much that can usefully be said about temperament because it's something we're all born with and there's very little we can do about it. Yet many aspiring top-rankers in table tennis as well as other games shy away from the word as though it were a deadly disease. The fact is that at top-level, all and every kind of temperament is to be seen on display in table tennis. Some players, such as Johansson of Sweden behave like perfect gentlemen. Others shout and almost rave, and are even liable to go off the court if things go badly for them. When certain players are really wound up, they have to find a safety valve of some kind. Stipancic of Yugoslavia is a perfect example. I have often found myself all set to serve a ball to him only to find that while I have been recovering the ball and getting set, he has gone wandering off to have a word with his captain. Some players cannot play a single point without having to towel off.

The Chinese are the best disciplined and least temperamental of all the players. The Japanese are anything but inscrutable Orientals when it comes to table tennis; they get very excited and jump up and down and run about a lot. But in general, it is the Europeans who betray the most temperament. The famous Swede, Hans Alser, was possibly the greatest gamesman I have ever encountered. He moaned about everything – about noise, about spectators moving about. I used to complain that if a number forty-nine bus went past four blocks away, he'd moan about that. So the player who worries unduly about an unruly temperament should stop worrying about it; some of the world's best players at present behave in a most extreme form, and seem none the worse for it. The fact is that if you are nervous and keyed up, and in any big tournament you are bound to be both, there is no harm in letting off steam. You will be more popular and more respected, perhaps, if you bottle things up inside you. But if your main aim is to win then, much as I dislike giving the advice, you are entitled to employ whatever mental crutch suits you as an individual.

Perhaps no word annoys me more than the word "concentration". Time and again I have heard sports commentators on T.V. and radio pontificate about a player's concentration – "he didn't concentrate on that one", "he lost his concentration there" and so on. All this is codswallop. Players at top level in almost any sport never lose their concentration, certainly when engaged in an important match. Nor is there any particular trick to blotting out extraneous noises or disturbances, visual or otherwise. The only time a player is likely to "lose his concentration" or to be upset by noise or movement around him is when his opponent is presenting him with a particularly stiff battle. Watch a good player when he is well on top: you could drop an atom bomb outside the front door and he would never bat an eyelid. That same player when up against a better will throw a tantrum if somebody in the back row of the stadium as much as coughs.

I know from personal experience that when you are under stress, you do and need to do silly things. When I get very keyed up I'll wander about the playing area, chatting to my friends in the front seats or 'having a go' at the umpire. Some players, such as Trevor Taylor, the Commonwealth champion, can be put off their game by the slightest disturbance. In my view, advice is useless. Your game is not likely to be improved if you bite on your tongue and suppress your true feelings. On the whole, and always within bearable limits, I'm in favour of players allowing their feelings to surface if they feel they need to carry on their game.

Temperament and concentration are red herrings in any serious discussion of the mental equipment you must bring to the table tennis table. Nobody, in my opinion, tries to *lose* their concentration. Generally, you are simply beaten by a better shot or by a better player. If, for any reason, you do happen to nod, there is nothing you can do about it. You have nodded, and that's that. Certainly there are no mental exercises known to me or anyone else which would help you to overcome a tendency towards loss of concentration.

It can happen, of course, if you are up against an opponent who is far too good for you or if you are playing somebody who is much inferior. Then the reason for a lack of concentration would be simple boredom – and the remedy for that is obvious. Don't play people who are far too good for you except to pick up tips. Avoid those who can't give you a real game, unless you are keen to impart some of your knowledge and experience to up and coming players which is a good thing to do.

Psychological play is as important in table tennis as in any other sport. You are, up against two opponents every time you play a game – the man opposite you and yourself. You can, in fact, easily beat yourself. By this, I mean, that your own mental approach may be all wrong. To give you the simplest example: I have known some of the best players in the world lose control of their game simply because they have been niggled by a bad decision of the umpire. The first thing you must do is to put the bad breaks out of your mind and concentrate upon the next points. If you allow yourself to be upset when your opponent gets a lucky and undeserved point, you will merely lose more points you should have won.

Psychological play has been brought to such a fine art in table tennis at the top level that in certain cases it borders not only on gamesmanship but outright cheating. One has to deprecate some of the unsporting things that are done in international circles and console oneself that unsporting play is common in most games today.

There are, however, legitimate ways of 'psyching' an opponent in order to put him off his game. Indeed, the whole purpose of different bats and different strokes is to surprise your opponent or force him into error and if you put him at a disadvantage mentally, you are perfectly entitled to do so.

At international level, a careful survey of your potential opponents is made by your coach. National squads study video-recordings of their op-

Stanislav Gomozkov from Russia demonstrating that he has the best backhand in the world

ponents' games, looking for weaknesses in skill or temperament. For instance, the English national coach will have noted that the great Swede Johansson does not like a short service to his backhand. But there are a few simple hints that can be useful to almost anyone playing short of international level.

There is no harm in mentally unsettling your opponent, or not allowing him to settle down. Some players like to start talking to you, presumably with the intention of distracting you or perhaps needling you. Personally I never get involved in chat with any of my opponents.

If your opponent favours a quick game, if he likes to get on with the game, then it is quite legitimate to try and slow the game down between points, thus causing him to lose control of himself through frustration. This is the kind of psychological warfare adopted in particular by the Hungarians and Czechs. If you show the slightest signs of impatience they will play on that — wandering off between points to chat to their captain or talk to their friends or indulge in some other kind of unnecessary business.

On the other hand, if you happen to take five quick points in a row after a tremendous exertion of energy, they will rush for the ball and try to get the game restarted as quickly as possible to take advantage of that moment when you naturally want to relax a little after your big effort. You ought to be on guard for this — a good moment, in fact, to do some towelling yourself. But find some excuse. In this way you will not only give yourself a chance to get your own wind back but contribute to your opponent's frustration.

There are all sorts of variations of the psychological approach and each player should study his opponent as the game proceeds and look for little ways of disturbing his natural rhythm. Nor is there any reason why you shouldn't lure your opponent into a state of complacency. It is sometimes a good idea not to reveal your best shots too soon but to reserve them for a really critical moment in a game. For instance, some of the best shakehand servers in the game such as Gomozkov of Russia will wait until the score has reached nineteen-all before suddenly turning on the heat. By this stage, you think you have mastered his serve; but suddenly he will deliver the unplayable stroke.

Surprise, therefore, is very often the key to success. It is worth remembering to keep something up your sleeve for the moment when you really need a winner.

SHOTS
AND
TACTICS○

BASIC GRIPS○

The two basic grips in modern table tennis are the shakehand and the penhold. The first is frequently called the Western style; the penhold grip only became a part of the world table tennis scene with the arrival of competitors from Asia.

Nothing, of course, could be more old-fashioned than the penhold grip which dates back to the early days of ping-pong. But as the modern game developed, with its emphasis on speed, aggression and athleticism, European players tended to find it artificial, even amateurish; it was the way maiden aunts played. Instead they went for the much more virile and natural grip – the shakehand; which means exactly what it says – one grips the bat the way that one would shake hands.

There are, of course, individual variations. I find that I sometimes turn my index finger round the edge of the racquet and depending on the shot I intend to play, also move my thumb around. My grip, therefore, is not entirely static; it changes with the tempo of the game I'm playing or more particularly, with the kind of game my opponent is attempting to play. I grip my racquet right up to the blade. I feel that in this way it becomes more an extension of my arm than a tool. But many players who favour a lot of wrist action, grasp the bat at the very end of the handle. The best advice I can give you is to experiment for yourself. You must seek to do what comes most naturally. I can only tell you how I achieve my own best results – but I know several players of world class whose grip is different from mine. There is even a Japanese player – his name is Hasegawa – who breaks all the rules. He takes hold of the bat in the Western style but sticks his index finger straight up the centre of the blade. To muddle all his opponents, he then proceeds to play as though he were using the penhold grip. This is a mixture of styles and grips which certainly works admirably for him, but not for others.

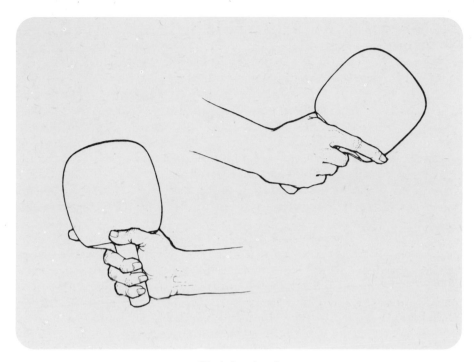

Shakehand grip

No one – literally no one – in world class table tennis used anything but the shakehand grip until those dramatic moments when the Japanese descended on the game in the early 1950s. For the better part of twenty years, the penhold grip dominated international table tennis and every world champion until 1971 used it. Like the shakehand grip, the word itself explains the grip; penhold is simply the way most people use a pen. My own belief is that its popularity with the Japanese, and later the Chinese, is dependent, not on pens, but on chopsticks, From childhood, both Japanese and Chinese are taught to use chopsticks the way we use a knife and fork. I can think of nothing more natural than that they should hold a table tennis bat the way they would hold chopsticks. And, of course, the handshake has never been a custom native to Asia.

The really astonishing thing is that the Asians were capable of producing world champions using what, on the face of it, appears such a very restrictive grip. Most of them place their thumb and index finger on the front of the racquet, with the rest of their fingers spread out like a fan on the rear side. Again, astonishingly, more than ninety per cent of all Japanese players never use the rear side of their bats at all, never play a backhand shot. Itoh was one of the exceptions. He would play most of his rallies with his forehand but then abruptly hit with the natural rubber on the rear in order to get a funny bounce which would usually fox you. Many of the Japanese players have nothing but the plain wood on the reverse side of the bat – which doesn't stop one or two of them unexpectedly playing a stroke with the rear which usually produces a shot with no life in it; the ball will simply drop over the net. On the whole, however, the Japanese are content to rely entirely on speed, agility, spin and physical fitness.

They play on percentages. They have worked it out that their kamikaze tactics must inevitably bring them victory. Out of every fifteen strokes they deliver, they reckon that if five go off the table, at least ten will be pure winners. This does not suit the Western mentality; Western players prefer to play every point on its merits. The Japanese, on the other hand, believe that they should hit every ball as hard as possible.

Most of us found it difficult to imagine that we were ever likely to see more skilful or aggressive proponents of the penhold style than the Japanese. But in 1959 the Chinese emerged to startle the world with some of the most fantastic players I have ever seen. Their penhold grip was not quite the same as that used by the Japanese. They did not use the fan but bunched their fingers close together. I have emphasised the speed and agility of the Japanese but in comparison with the Chinese they seemed slow and sluggish. Japanese players, contrasting them purely with the Chinese, relied mainly on spin and terrific smashes. The greatest asset the Chinese had on the other hand, was their sheer ability to cover ground. They were cat-like both in speed and accuracy. Their style was completely their own. Probably the greatest player I have ever seen was Chuang Tse-Tung who won the world title in 1961, 1963 and 1965. Normally, as I've said, penhold grip players rarely use the backhand. Chuang amazed everybody by using a backhand, although unlike Western players who use the rear-side of the bat to make a stroke, Chuang manoeuvred his arm and wrist in such a way that his backhand stroke was played with the forehand side of his bat. This was a truly astonishing stroke!

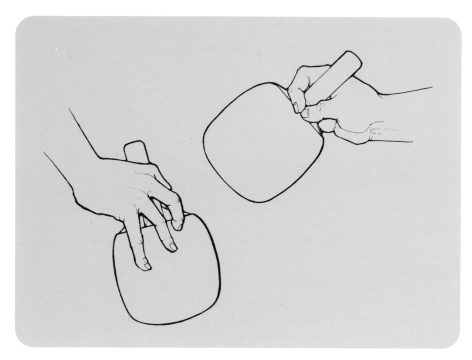

Penhold grip

Controversy has raged for several years now as to the relative merits of the two grips. It says much for European stubbornness and tenacity that despite the Japanese and Chinese successes, Western players persevered with their shakehand. In my opinion, they had little choice in the matter. Given a Westerner's height, weight and general inability to move as quickly as smaller and lighter men, the shakehand grip is the only possible grip for anybody of Caucasian stock. In another way, too, it was always inevitable that the shakehand grip must, in the end, defeat the penhold. Even five years ago one had only to watch a game between a skilled shakehand player and a penhold gripper to see how the shakehand player *ought* to have won the game. The shakehander could remain in the centre of the table and dominate play with his terrific backhand, making the penhold gripper rush about all over the place.

The primary reason for the success of the Asians had nothing to do with grip, anyhow. It depended almost entirely on the fact that the

Asians were more acrobatic than their Western opponents. Yet the penhold grip, if you were built the right way to use it, offered two distinct advantages. With the shakehand, a player has to learn and practice *four* fundamental strokes while the penhold player has to master only *one*. Given the same amount of time for practice, this means that a penhold player gets four times as much practice making a shot in a particular style as a Westerner.

The penhold grip also allows a player to disguise his stroke better. As he waggles his bat back and forwards like a water diviner before actually hitting the ball, the Asian player finds it easier to mask the true direction both of his shot and the kind of spin he is intending to impart. Possibly the greatest of all Chinese players was Li Fu-Yung whose serve, in particular, it was impossible to read. When he waggled his bat, it was at such speed that you never knew which side he was going to use or whether the spin was going to be topspin, sidespin or backspin. Hsu Yin-Sheng was almost as good – certainly he was the trickiest server the game has ever seen. He played one serve that went over the net and came right back to him. He had another serve where the ball once it bounced, then made a detour round your bat. Another great player was Chuang Shim-Lin who, although a defensive player, could impart a spin which nobody, not even the Japanese, could read.

I once had the idea that if I were starting to play table tennis all over again, I'd try and adapt myself to the penhold grip. I think many Western players have toyed with the idea. But in the last few years I've come to realise that it's not suitable for Europeans because of their physical build. It is agility that makes the grip work for the Far Easterners. Indeed, I have come to the conclusion that the importance of the grip has been overemphasised in table tennis anyway. In the last analysis, it is the player, his dedication, concentration, determination, his natural talent, that matter and not the way he holds his bat. Most top players agree with me.

What happens if you have started with a grip and want to change it? My advice is: don't bother. If you are Asian you are almost bound to follow the penhold tradition and seek some new technique to break the present Western supremacy. Rather, that is, than adapt to the shakehand which you are almost certain to find difficult.

If you are European, I do not believe there is any advantage in trying to beat the penhold champions with the penhold grip. However, if you have started with a penhold grip, then stick to it. The same goes for the shakehand grip.

Once you have learned a grip, you are really stuck with it. If you are reasonably proficient already with your present grip, if would be courting disaster to try and learn an entirely new technique by changing your grip. I have never heard of a first-class player attempting such a thing and I would strongly advise against any such tinkering. Time spent mastering the new grip would be better spent, in my opinion, perfecting your present techniques and mastering those skills in which you show the most promise.

THE
SERVICE○

The emphasis in table tennis is constantly shifting. New materials create new problems. New grips, players from new countries with new styles – all these things revolutionise the game, if only for a decade. Until recently, the serve in table tennis was not thought of as a match-winning stroke. It was used almost exclusively to get the game going. Today, a whole game can hinge on your skill with the service, and also on the way you return your opponent's serve.

The trick with the serve is to drop it very short, just over the net. I don't advise anybody to try and emulate Hsu who could make the ball bounce back over the net; that's a trick in a lifetime. The ball should be played with backspin and you get 'the right effect by tilting your bat forward and allowing your wrist to drop down about a foot. Variation is achieved by the speed with which your wrist drops; the faster you drop your wrist, the greater the spin. But a table can look vast and your opponent is trained to deal with service. So it is also important to consider exactly *where* to place your service. At top-level, I find it best to serve to your opponent's forehand because, extraordinarily, most players find it difficult to return from this angle. But the service is becoming so sophisticated in modern table tennis that few players would try the same service to the same spot with the same spin as a matter of routine.

At the root of your service should lie a little psychology. Remember that it is one of the few shots where you have complete choice as regards tempo, direction, speed, spin and variation. Your opponent's strengths may restrict your choice to some extent, yet it remains true that you are in complete command of the situation. You must always think carefully, therefore, before playing your stroke. If you think your opponent is expecting a *different* service, there is often no harm in repeating the same stroke exactly. But he must never be able really to guess your intentions.

Christian Martin, France, spin serving

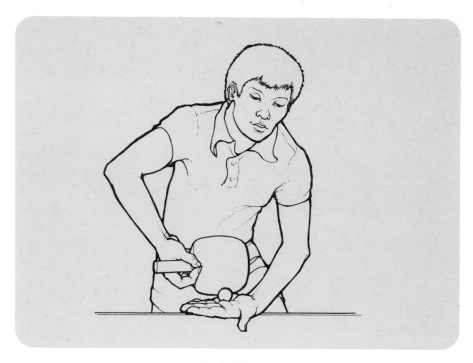

Penhold serve

Masking the service is one of the great arts of the game – although it belongs more in the penhold repertoire than the shakehand. The Chinese initially gave the shakehanders a great deal of trouble, and still do, because it is so difficult to read their intentions. Men like Chuang, Li and Hsu, whose services I have already described, placed the shakehanders at enormous disadvantage. Li and his successors brush the bat backwards and forwards so quickly that it is impossible to discover whether they are hitting the ball with top spin or backspin – or, indeed, any spin at all. This has proved one of the great advantages of the penhold grip. Even if you do manage to return the ball, and most players at least do this, the penhold players are all set for the kill at once. While it is possible to win points outright with the serve in table tennis, it still does not carry the significance of the big serve in lawn tennis. In the main, the purpose of the difficult service is to set up your opponent for the next attacking – and killer – stroke.

Melevoy Karakasevic from Yugoslavia, the best European penholder, spin serving

Shakehand serve

The shakehand grip, of course, also allows a skilful player an opportunity for masking what he is actually doing. For example, by placing the bat out to the side of your body at about chest height and then drawing it across your body very fast, you can impart tremendous side spin on the ball. You control the amount of spin you desire by the speed with which you draw your arm across your body. The two best servers using the shakehand grip – the only practical grip for a Westerner – are both Russian. Gomozkov and Sarkojan are outstanding. This might be because the Russians are rumoured to have developed a special machine for monitoring a table tennis serve.

The essence of their serve is that they throw the ball very very high. In itself, this tends to confuse you when you are playing them – do you keep your eye on the ball or on your man? If you don't watch the ball, exactly how late do you catch it? If you concentrate on it, at what point to you discover the amount of spin, direction and so on which is going to come over the net at you, matters which you can only anticipate by studying your opponent's posture, stance, distance from table, angle of his bat, projected length of his stroke and the other factors which you must take in at a flash in ordinary circumstances?

The higher you throw the ball, of course, the faster it comes down and the greater the impact you can secure when you strike the ball. The Russians are the only Westerners who can win points outright with their serve. Even Jonyer of Hungary, the world's Number 1 rarely if ever wins outright on service. Most shakehanders are content to serve short – a tremendous art in itself, of course – forcing their opponents to scramble the ball back over the net somehow or other and leaving them wide open to a loop and forehand smash. (See pages 51-68.)

RETURNING SERVICE○

The push stroke is so fundamental that most players, even those comparatively new to the game, tend to take it for granted. The trouble is that it doesn't look *spectacular* and most players like winning with something that looks good. Certainly there is a psychological gain in making a tremendous looking shot. It not only enhances your own morale, but saps your opponent's. Yet at advanced table tennis levels, players have long ago learned to ignore window-dressing. In their book what counts is the shot that wins a point. And a push can win you a point after a tough service or long rally just as easily as brilliant forehand loop. The fundamental importance of the push stroke, however, is that it is the one stroke you have in your repertoire that allows you to return service successfully if you've been left in a position from which you yourself cannot launch an attack.

Return of service is so essential to your game that it repays every moment of practice and concentrated thought you can give it. To make the push stroke, therefore, tilt the bat slightly at an angle, pushing it forward and down for about ten inches but making certain that the bat is kept under the ball at all times.

A forehand stroke is always taken just off the body, a backhand in front of it. Despite this, if you find it difficult to return your opponent's service, your best bet is to play for the centre of the table, which allows you the greatest margin for error. You should, of course, be concentrating your attention on the amount of spin your opponent is attempting to impart to the ball; misreading spin will cause you as much trouble as anything you are likely to face. Your opponent, of course, will make shots about which you can do nothing; in such cases you have to learn to suffer the loss of a point, not worry about it or allow it to niggle you and get on with the job of winning the point back. In other words,

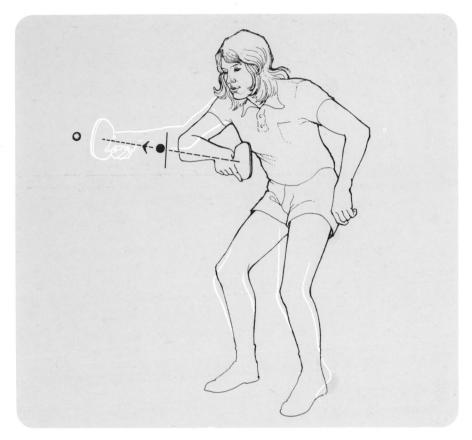

Push stroke — backhand return of service

returning service is a part of the game about which you can take positive and effective steps.

Always try to place the ball so that your opponent cannot set up a forehand attack. For all servers except the Russians, some of the Chinese and Japanese, the whole purpose of the shot is to force you to make a silly return, opening the way to allowing them to get their attack going. So place the ball deep, or just over the net. Leaving it midway down the table is simply to invite disaster.

Again, never take your opponent's service for granted. Guile is as much a part of top table tennis as anything else. A good player such as

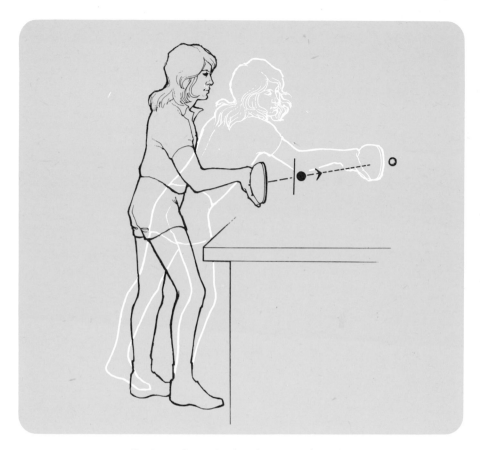

Push stroke — forehand return of service

Bengtsson of Sweden will often tempt you into believing you have mastered his service. Then, when he needs a point desperately, either to retrieve a position or to break through into his own attack, he will produce an unexpected service that will leave you floundering. So never take your eye off the ball or get over-confident. The chances are that if you do, your return will be a sucker shot and your opponent will take ample advantage.

I have explained that the Chinese, in particular, are masters of the service — one of the real advantages of the penhold grip — some of them such as Hsu being able to turn the ball as much as two feet when they serve.

This is largely because his grip allows the Asian to turn his bat in a half circle and thus gives him greater flexibility. Yet I was able to master the Chinese services. I did this by keeping on the alert, never blinking an eyelid, studying my opponent's moves, expecting any and every variation and being prepared for it.

Even at top level, there are three basic rules to remember:

Keep your eye both on the ball and your opponent's bat to judge the spin. Study the angle of the bat and the projected length of stroke – how far back does he bring his arm?

Aim to play down the centre line if you are unfamiliar with your opponent's play or believe he is foxing.

When you feel you have mastered his service, keep him on the run by varying your return – always aiming either for the deep backhand or just over the net.

THE PUSH STROKE IN PLAY○

Although the push stroke is your basic shot for returning an opponent's service it can be used very effectively throughout the whole range of the game. Some attacking players – Bengtsson of Sweden, Georgiuca of Roumania and Miko of Yugoslavia – use it simply as a sparring move to allow them an opportunity to get their attack going. Others, such as the women players, Jill Hammersley and Alexandru of Roumania who are strictly defensive players, keep pushing and pushing until their opponent makes a mistake and drives into the net or off the table. Whatever you might think of such a tactic many of the greatest world stars employ it – particularly those I have mentioned above – happy to keep pushing the ball back over the net for as long as fifteen minutes when the *Expedite* rule comes into force – the equivalent of the lawn tennis *Tie-break*. This rule makes it obligatory that the server must win a point within twelve strokes. (See page 107.)

Even players whose game is not naturally defensive use the push a lot. I've seen some of the best – Bengtsson and Johansson for instance, keep it up for fifteen minutes without losing a point, arguing that it puts a fine edge on their concentration and enables them to get "in touch" with the game. Every player has his own preference about these things, however, and I can only recommend that you experiment with the push and see how best you can suit it to your own style of play. I suggest you try it out with an opponent and see if you can both keep it up for ten minutes without either missing the ball.

One more point: never hurry a push stroke; take it easy and concentrate not only on keeping the ball on the table but as near your opponent's end-line as possible. Personally I always use a very short action when I'm making a push stroke. But my idea fundamentally is to open out the game and allow me to bring in my attacking repertoire. The

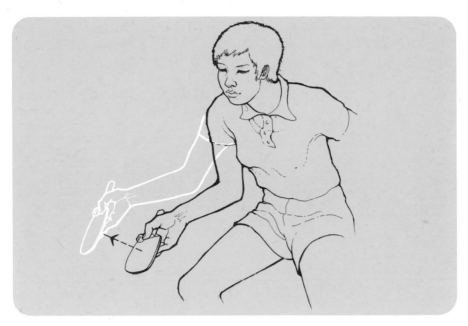

Push stroke – penholder's version

players who favour attack play – the vast majority of table tennis stars these days – use the same short action. To attack well, you need to stand closer to the table than the defensive player with the result that your action is bound to be shorter in general. Yet it is interesting to watch two players, both from the same country, Sweden, who are essentially attacking players but who manage to vary their action. Bengtsson plays a short, sharp stroke while his compatriot Johansson's stroke is almost three times as long. On the whole, I think Bengtsson does better out of the push.

When you face a penhold player, you have to re-think all your ideas about the push. They employ what to us in the West seems a very funny stroke. Their push looks more like a simple block. They push the ball forward quite straight and with no tilt to the bat but they take the ball very very quickly off the table. The shot has little or no spin. What they are relying on is that their sheer speed, accuracy and lack of spin will give an opponent no chance to do anything with the ball and indeed, most of us are usually content not to lose a point here, never mind making an attempt to play a winner. The great exponents of this shot are Itoh, Immano and the woman player, Matsuzaki; with the men in particular, the shots used to come raining at you so fast that it was like having to play a game composed entirely of half-volleys.

The drawback of relying too heavily on the push is that you can be so easily tripped up by the *Expedite* rule. This requires that, if a rally lasts for fifteen minutes, then each player must take it in turn to serve, and must win a point within twelve strokes. The rule is important in making the game more spectacular. Long defensive rallies are boring both for players and spectators alike. Some players faced with this frustrating push, push, push defensive play, change their own attacking style and simply return tit for tat until they force the *Expedite* rule to be invoked. In which case, of course, the purely defensive player *has* to hit out and invariably, because this is foreign to his or her game, loses a point.

THE
FOREHAND○

The forehand attack, for many years the most important stroke in the game, still largely retains its supremacy although some players would argue that a good service is gradually catching up with it in significance. Nonetheless, the fact remains that if all services were to become unplayable, table tennis would cease. So however short and sharp the modern rally, a player still faces the problem of what to do after his or her opponent has returned service successfully or a player has made a successful return himself. I used to advise that there were several different kinds of forehand drive but I now consider that they can all be reduced to a basic five. These are straightforward forehand drives, but the angle of the bat can be made different or the shot can be played from or to a different position or simply played in a different way.

Some players like Bengtsson favour a short swing; others like Johansson like to stand fairly upright and use a longer stroke; some like Dennis Neale of England, master of this particular shot, favour a flat drive or one with top spin or even side spin. Some players like to mix up their strokes to bewilder their opponents. This particularly applies to the world Number 1, Jonyer of Hungary.

For the basic action of the forehand drive, a top player stands with his right foot slightly behind his left and his body slightly sideways on to the table. The bat should be held poised about eighteen inches out from your side and just below hip height. The arm is then brought straight up with the elbow slightly bent, and the bat should carry through right up past your head. It is this upward action that puts spin on the ball, making it rise up over the net and bringing it down, still spinning, safely on the other side and not off the table. This is the normal forehand drive and you can clear the net by as much as you like with it because if you've got the right spin on it, it will come down without fail once it is over. A

Former World Champion Stellan Bengtsson of Sweden has a powerful forehand game

good height to aim at, in fact, is six inches which allows plenty of margin for error.

The best topspin player – the man with the best forehand drive in the world – is undoubtedly Jonyer, closely followed by the French and European champion, Secretin. Jonyer occasionally plays the shot with a tremendous sidespin just to vary the stroke and unsettle your game; you have to watch the ball with an eagle-eye when you're up against him for it can break so sharply that you will miss it altogether. Another player who is very difficult to play when he uses his forehand drive is Stipancic of Yugoslavia; the problem here is that Stipancic is a left-hander so that when he spins the ball, you've got to try and remember that everything is

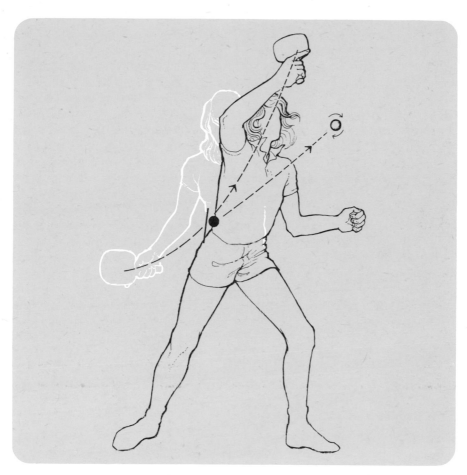

Forehand drive

in reverse. You have to be really on your toes with him, of course, because he can play with an almost equally good backhand.

Played by a master, the forehand drive looks, and often is, an unplayable stroke. The penhold players in particular favour this method of execution. Ogimura of Japan was possibly the most terrifying opponent when you offered him a chance. He would hit the ball with such force that it would bounce way up in the air and there was so much power and weight behind the stroke that he could not help performing a pirouette.

Having made a good forehand drive, your next worry is how your opponent is going to handle it. Almost certainly he is going to chop. If he likes to bring his bat down fast, you have to increase the height of your follow through in order to impart more spin and so counteract your opponent's coming chop, or return it. You can always drop the speed a bit if you discover that your opponent is chopping very lightly; everything, in fact, depends upon how you read his chop because once you have got the weight of it, you should be able to roll forehand topspins all evening.

At top level, one always aims to take the ball at the top of the bounce because this obviously gives you more of the far side of the table to aim at. Once you begin to let the ball drop, you have to increase your topspin in order to clear the net successfully, but still keeping it on the table.

Jonyer and Stipancic achieve the perfection they do through timing and technique. The only sensible and practical advice I could give you would be to practise and practise and practise . . . Great musicians have always perfected and retained their enormous skills through practice. The same thing goes for table tennis.

Differences in racquets, of course, tend to make for differences in how a forehand drive is played. A reverse bat will give more spin (and allow the ball to clear the net at greater height) than a dimpled rubber. Different national squads hit differently, too – the Russians Gomozkov and Sarkojan are inclined to "slap" the ball – that is, they bring the bat across the face on the follow through, while the Swedes favour a longer follow-through.

Among the tips I would give are:

Don't stand too square – otherwise you will lose sight of the ball as it comes to your bat.

When playing forehand against drop or push, the angle of the bat should be almost upright as this allows you to get more spin on the ball.

When you are playing a counter-hitter (see under *Counter-attack*) tilt the angle of the bat slightly forward which allows you to hit flatter and to neutralise your opponent's spin, but keep a watchful eye open for any change of spin by your opponent.

If your opponent suddenly puts a chop ball in, switch your bat straight up. If he counter-hits, tilt the bat slightly forward.

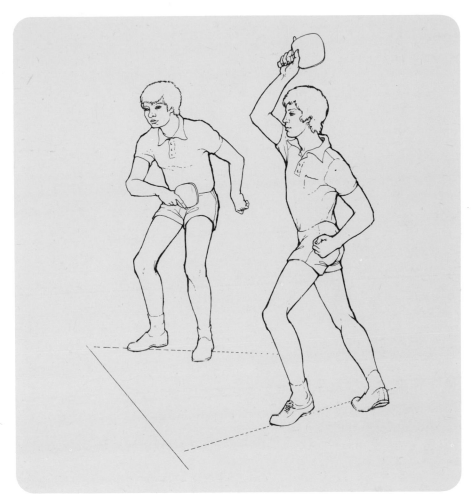

Forehand drive – playing position

There are more sophisticated variations of the forehand drive. For example, there is the forehand chop smash, very useful if the ball comes to you very high and near the net when it can be chopped down just over the far side. This stroke is very much the equivalent of the overhead smash in lawn tennis – I've seen Ogimura of Japan smash his ball down with such force that it has bounced twenty feet in the air! But be careful:

Forehand drive — top spin

make sure the ball is high and near the net. A deep ball is useless; you'll almost certainly drive it out.

The sidespin smash should also be attempted only when the ball is high and near the net. Take your bat well above your head, then bring it down and across. The spin should take the ball away from your opponent. However, there is a tendency among modern players to spot what you are up to very quickly and they generally move in and across with tremendous speed to cut the ball off before it can begin to swerve away.

A shot I favour personally is one straight down the right-hand line of the table. I bring my left shoulder back and push my arm more away from my body. Incidentally, never rush any of these shots; be patient. I've often hit a ball across the net sixty times before attempting a winner. Also always watch the ball right on to your bat and if it comes well up, hit it as hard and firmly as you can.

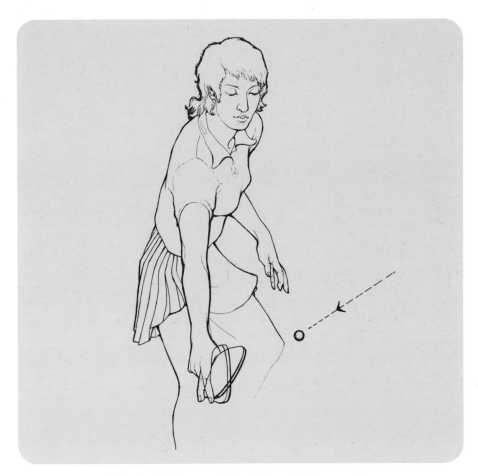

Forehand drive – tilting bat against counterhit

Your game must always vary with that of your opponent. If he is small, you can afford to swing the ball about wide. If he's tall, hit it straight down the middle at his person. Even if he gets in a return, he'll be so tied up that he ought to have no chance with your follow-up. Playing against Johansson of Sweden, for example, you never knock the ball wide. If you do, you'll get a terrific forehand back. The way to play him is to shoot the ball down the middle which invariably ties him up. With Bengtsson on the other hand, the middle ball is useless. He's small and quick and gets his body out of the way with remarkable agility. Indeed, with his short, sharp action, there's nothing he likes better than to stand in the centre of the table and swap centre-line shots with you. The only way to play him, in fact, is to drive wide, making him stretch or run.

I'm very much in favour of the drop shot when somebody has a good rhythm of forehand drives going against you. Too often when an opponent has been forced well away from the table, a player will fail to take his opportunity and instead of merely dropping the ball just over the net, continues his full-blooded drives. Even where an opponent manages to catch your drop, the effort lays him wide open to your next return. It is a particularly useful shot when you are playing a defensive player. However, only attempt a drop when a defensive player has made a bad short return. Also, always hit it back to his vulnerable side if he does manage to return it. If his stroke is a forehand, drive it to his backhand and vice versa, for when he's close in he will find it difficult to change sides. If, on the other hand, your own drop shot is a bad one, be on your toes for a smash return. If you're lucky and have more or less taken your opponent's measure, you'll probably know which side he favours for the smash and you will have put your shot to his weakest side.

THE
LOOP○

The loop still remains the greatest stroke in modern table tennis. Basically it's a forehand drive, but with a tremendous amount of extra topspin. It is best used against a chop or a ball with backspin.

Jonyer, Secretin and some other top players when looping, never take the ball at the top of the bounce, as the best coaches tell you to do. Instead, they take the ball when it is dropping. Indeed, they take the ball very, very low, well below the knee and they achieve a terrific spin by brushing the ball in the lightest possible way, then follow through to the maximum.

I should warn that the loop is only for really good players. An average club player trying out the shot, for example, is almost certain to miss the ball. At least at first. He shouldn't worry, however; even Jonyer, when he first began, missed the ball. With practice, however, the shot becomes possible. It does wreck your normal game for a while, in particular your normal forehand. But the good player who wants to become an advanced player has to persevere with it and in the end will find that once he has thoroughly mastered the loop, his normal forehand skills will gradually return.

There are many different ways of employing the loop. There is the dummy loop which I personally favour. I pretend I'm going to play a full loop but instead I put much less spin on the ball. Nine times out of ten this will fool my opponent. Like most competitive players I try to mix my shots.

The dummy loop is one of the most advanced strokes in the repertoire. Only when you are a master of the shot should you try and extend your range to this level.

Some players achieve much the same result by turning their racquet round. In particular Danny Seemiller of America is well known for this

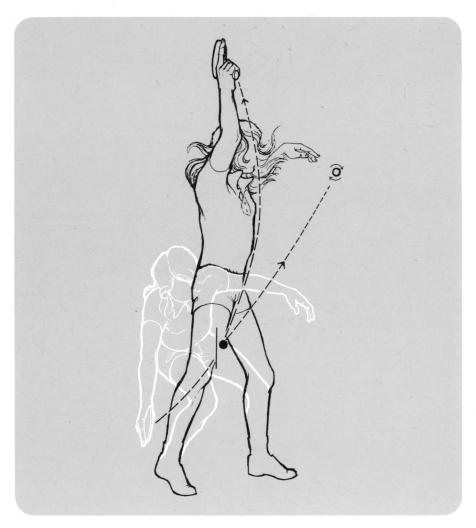

High loop taken low

ploy. He hits very fast with one side of his bat, then he suddenly reverses it and because he had different rubber on the reverse, he produces a very much slower return. He plays exactly the same shot, but it comes across with little or no spin. And he's such a master of disguise that he can turn the racquet in his hand usually without you noticing it.

Anton Stipancic, Yugoslavia, playing a forehand loop

Both Seemiller and Hasegawa are among the most impressive loopers I've ever seen. Both shoot over very fast loops. Hasegawa in particular shoots the ball just over the net and it flies through really low. Because of his very supple body – he can turn from the hips very well – he can change direction with his loop very swiftly.

Orlowski of Czechoslovakia is probably the greatest exponent of the high loop in the game today. He will stand something like 30 feet (9 metres) back from the table, take the ball very low and produce a beautiful high loop that crosses the net like a flying bomb. In the high loop, the ball comes at you spinning and wobbling and moving apparently quite slowly. But it's a desperately difficult ball to play, if only

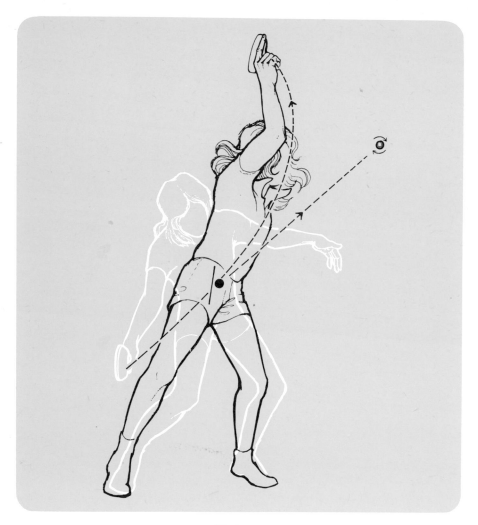

High loop

because you find yourself caught in two minds as how to play it. With most shots, you have no time to think and so you rely almost completely on your reflexes. With the high loop, you seem to have all the time in the world to decide what to do which can often be fatal. Watch out for the return, though, when you use the loop. Remember that your opponent

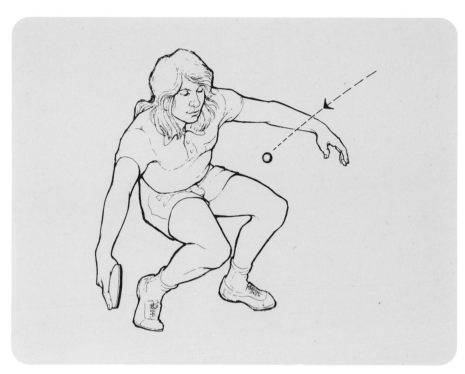

Starting low for looping the loop

will have reversed your spin; or if it's somebody like Jonyer, it may come back at you with both top and sidespin on it and will break as soon as it hits the table, either in towards you or perhaps wide of your bat. When up against a skilful looper, you've got to be ready to take the ball at any angle and breaking any way.

At the top level the loop has been refined beyond all knowledge; so much, indeed, that the very best loopers play a stroke called looping the loop. This simply means that each player loops the ball back at his opponent. But to loop the ball and then get a loop back is an extraordinary experience. The ball strikes your bat with a jarring kick. The great exponents are Jonyer, Georgiuca, Gergely of Hungary and Secretin. When such players start looping the loop the spectator is watching table tennis at its most spectacular and breathtaking. The players in some cases stand a full 60 feet (18 metres) away from the table. The ball comes over

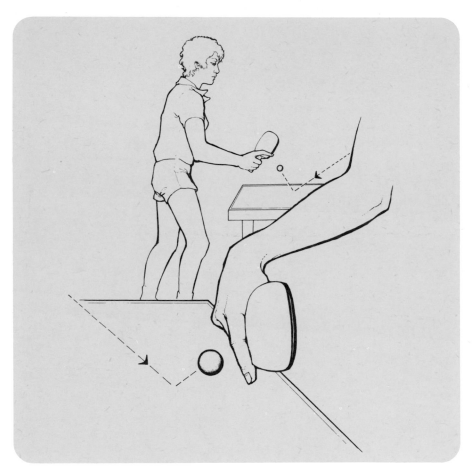

Half-volley block, fore and backhand

spinning, whirling, wobbling very high and very fast. The players will allow it almost to reach the floor, hoping, of course, that the lower it drops, the less spin it will retain, before giving it the lightest but speediest brush imaginable whereupon it goes soaring back. It is almost impossible to try a drop shot in these circumstances although with an opponent a full sixty feet behind the table, a drop shot seems the sensible solution. The fact is that speed and spin will defeat any such attempt. If

World Champion Istvan Jonyer of Hungary ending a backhand loop — one of the great shots in modern table tennis

you do attempt a drop shot, also, you'll invariably find that you have un-
wittingly telegraphed your intention and a player of Secretin's calibre,
for example, will move in like a cat and murder you.

You need very supple wrists to play a good backhand loop. One of the
best in the world at the moment is the young coloured English lad Desmond Douglas of Birmingham. He has a lovely loose wrist movement
which gives him enormous power.

What, then, is the best way to play *against* a loop?

The classic answer – and both Douglas and Seemiller are past
masters of the art – is simply to block the ball, a stroke which is known as
the half-volley block. Tilt the bat forward, take the ball as soon as it
bounces; but make sure you are close to the table, and simply let the ball
hit your bat. This kills the spin before it has time to develop properly.
The angle of your bat largely depends on the amount of spin you are
meeting. Touch the ball softly – but watch out for a dummy loop! If you
think you're up against a dummy, then help the ball back by putting in
your half-volley a bit more firmly. If I find that my opponent's spin is
giving me trouble, I keep the ball as short as possible, which at least has
the effect of stopping him looping. By stopping the ball from coming off
the table, you can close up the game and wait for a chance to use your
own loop.

Where do you place your return loop? Most players find that it is comparatively easy just to block on the backhand but that the instinctive
reaction when the ball comes to your forehand is to loop back. You have
only two ways to go – and you'll soon find that if you drive back down
the forehand side of the table that the ball will overshoot. You really
have no option but to swing it across the table towards your opponent's
deep forehand. If, for any reason this is not possible, then another shot is
straight down the middle, thus presenting your opponent with a difficult
choice, for he won't know whether to use his forehand or backhand.
There's a good chance he'll muff the shot, and give you a chance to get
back on the attack yourself.

The loop, of course, tends to drive you away from the table, and if
you're an attacking player – and these days you're almost bound to be –
this is something you cannot afford to put up with. The answer is often
simply to let the spinning ball hit your bat, and watch it go back with a
very funny spin! I'm not talking about *cushioning* the impact; the best
analogy I can think of is to compare it with the way you catch a high

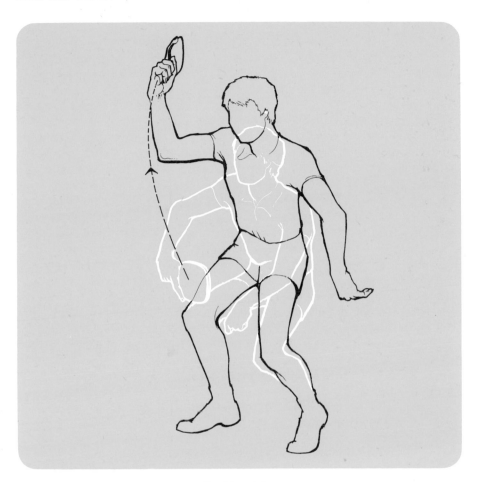

Backhand loop

cricket ball. If you haven't yet learned the trick, try putting your bat out firmly to start with and watch how the ball flies about. Gradually you'll learn to gauge the impact and the degree of cushioning needed to deaden the ball. And a good idea, always, is to play back down the middle of the table.

To summarize then: to play against the loop, try a half-volley block or better, if you can manage it, attempt to cushion the ball. Keep an eye out for the dummy loop, however!

One of the best new shots in the modern game, of course, is the backhand loop. The first man to demonstrate this with any marked success was the great Swede, Hans Alser. Essentially the shot looks like a normal backhand. But the trick, of course, as with the forehand loop, is to get very much greater spin. I ought to warn that it's an extremely difficult shot to play and even world-class players often miss it.

Your bat should start lower than usual and finish very much higher up. Once perfected, of course, the stroke opens out your opponent's game without you having to run around trying to get your forehand loop in. The world's greatest exponent of the shot is Jonyer who's so good that he can even backloop an ordinary topspin ball. The trouble for your opponent is that he has greater difficulty judging the spin from a backhand loop than from a normal forehand loop. What you have to do is to flick your wrist much more – but this is usually executed so quickly that your opponent has no time to measure the amount of your spin.

The shot is usually played relatively slowly and the ball delivered high over the net to allow for the greatest possible margin of error. As with the high loop already described, a good backhand loop can put your opponent in two minds; he never knows whether to try a straight block or whether to try an attack. Whichever he choses, he generally leaves himself wide open. A good idea is to backhand loop down your opponent's forehand side which gives him a great deal of trouble if he elects to try and block back.

Incidentally, as with the forehand loop, the backhand loop plays merry hell with your shoulder muscles.

COUNTER ATTACK○

In most games of table tennis, the counter-attack is the most prominent phase of the game. Many games are almost entirely devoted to it. Put simply, counter-attack merely means that when you attack an opponent, he returns the offensive immediately and both of you throw all defensive ideas to the wind.

In these days of big hitters and players who like spectacular points, counter-attack dominates. Jonyer with his great backhand loop, Surbek with his fitness and fighting spirit, Johansson with his half-vollies and tremendous forehand smash and Bengtsson with his extraordinary reflexes are among the game's master counter-hitters. Perhaps the best of the shakehanders as counter-hitters are Johansson and Dennis Neale of England who stand much closer to the table than the loopers and favour a short, sharp action. Among the penholders, the Japanese favour the loop which in general means less counter-hitting. The Chinese, on the other hand, are nearly all great counter-hitters.

The counter-attack forehand is similar to the standard forehand drive, the main difference being the angle at which you hold your bat. You should, if possible, take the ball very early off the table instead of waiting to take it at the top of the bounce. If you want to return very hard, step back a pace to give yourself plenty of room to get in your stroke. If your opponent chops at you, instead of beginning the stroke with the bat alongside your body, place it just behind your body at the side and tilt it a little more forward to give a forehand topspin. The bat has to be brought forward to counteract the spin your opponent has put on the ball and allow you to impart topspin yourself. But look out for a flat forehand. Give yourself plenty of time to adjust your own shot to what is likely to come over the net.

One way of "forecasting" what is likely to come at you is to have a

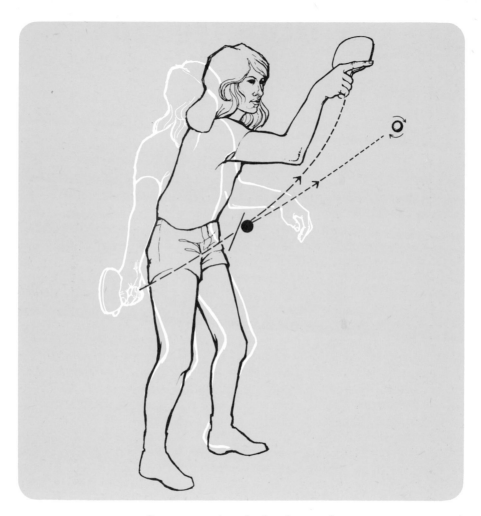

Counter-attack — forehand top spin

good look at the bat your opponent is using. If he is using a pimple (or
dimple) sandwich rubber or even a plain dimple, you will have to give
the ball a lot more air. So if you take his shot too early, you'll drive the
ball into the net. The reason is that dimpled bats generally put less spin
on the ball and tend to pull it down into the net. So remember to lift the
bat a little more and follow through much more purposefully.

Kjell Johannsson, Sweden, backhand counterhitting

The backhand counter-hit should operate with the speed and ferocity of a machine gun. You can, in fact, play a backhand counter-hit in no more than six inches of movement by using your wrist. This is why Desmond Douglas of England, although still not one of the best players in the world, is widely reckoned a menace by players who are technically his all-round superiors. Forehand or backhand, he takes everything on the half-volley. In general, the two greatest shakehand counter-hitters are probably Orlowski of Czechoslovakia and Gomozkov of Russia. The latter is widely considered the best backhand counter-hitter in the West – his stroke is very short, indeed. He plays the shot square on, right in front of his body.

Play the shot in front of your body, therefore, letting the bat move forward and across with plenty of wrist movement. Usually when I play the shot I'm also waiting to get my forehand in, so I try a few easy strokes before suddenly stepping up the pace and getting myself round to bring my forehand into action. When Orlowski or Gomozkov play this stroke, their opponent is generally thrown back as soon as they hit harder and faster than they have been doing, and this, of course, gives them the opening they want to get their own forehand going.

Personally, I like to use a very flat backhand counter hit. This usually has the effect of making my opponent hit the ball into the net. If, on the other hand, he lifts it high in desperation, then I get in an easy kill.

But what if your opponent tries the same tactics? The answer is to use much more spin on the backhand and keep the ball high over the net, thus neutralising the flat ball which your opponent may have driven at you. The backhand topspin – Orlowski, Gomozkov, Dennis Neale, young Desmond Douglas are the great exponents of this shot – is really basic to this type of play. To do it, take the ball in front of your body, then lift up the bat and sweep it across about eighteen inches (45 cms) only. This may seem very very short – but remember that you are playing what is mainly a sparring stroke. You begin with the bat just above the table and face-on, then take it up in a half-circle. If you have to use the stroke against a chop, start lower and make the shot much longer than eighteen inches.

Nearly all the best players in the game today try to get their forehand in as soon as possible. They like to close the game up by hitting down the backhand side, which is why I think a sound backhand is really worth cultivating. It is astonishing that so many world-class players – mainly

Counter-attack — backhand top spin

the penholders — lack a proper backhand. They try to compensate for this efficiency by agility and peak fitness. But if they should be slightly under par physically, they can easily lose a game to a player who is technically inferior.

I've always found the backhand counter-attack one of my most important weapons. Once I played and defeated, the Japanese Itoh when he was world champion with this stroke. I had him running about all over the place. The really great world champions, among them Chuang Tse-Tung, have all had great backhands, and have all been great backhand counter-attackers.

You should not try and play a fierce backhand counter-hit. Always take the stroke at a steady pace waiting your chance to throw in the un-expectedly quick one which will drive back your opponent and allow you to start up your forehand. Never try, I repeat, to get too much out of the backhand counter-hit; try and make it the safest stroke that you have in your repertoire.

How do you protect yourself against the backhand counter-hit, however? The stroke is so short and so quick that your opponent can easily change direction at the very least moment and leave you gasping off balance. I suggest you play your shot wide down your opponent's backhand or down the centre of the table. From my experience, this is likely to tie up your opponent or even if he manages a return and open the way for your own forehand to get going.

DEFENSIVE PLAY○

Apart from Scholer of West Germany and Bonzi of Hungary, the purely defensive game has almost completely disappeared from men's world-class table tennis. To see defensive play at its best today, one has to watch the women's game where England's Jill Hammersley and Roumania's Alexandru, who plays a very heavy defensive chop, are past-mistresses of the craft.

It is not merely male chauvinism to say that the women's game has more or less stood still for almost two decades. All the innovations have taken place in men's table tennis and a woman player who modelled her game on the great past masters such as Barna, Bergmann and Leach would have no difficulty holding her own among the best in women's table tennis. The best shots, the best players, the best techniques, therefore, are to be found exclusively in the men's game and for my own part I cannot understand why more women players do not attempt to copy them. The argument in most sports is that women suffer a physical handicap. But I find it difficult to understand why this should be so in table tennis. A table tennis ball, after all, is among the lightest of objects. To hit a lawn tennis ball hard may require certain strength for the ball itself is pretty heavy, particularly when delivered at speed. But a table tennis ball scarcely requires great physical strength to make it travel. Nor have the Asian players, generally handicapped physically in comparison with their Western opponents, found any difficulty in out-hitting their larger and stronger opponents.

Anyone wishing to study advanced table tennis techniques, therefore, can more or less safely ignore the modern women's game. But in an age when the best of the modern players are only too anxious to show how hard and how fast they can hit the ball, it is often useful to know something of the defensive game. For instance, an old-fashioned chop

Jill Hammersley, European Women's Champion, performing a forehand chop. Her body tilts sideways and her eyes are fixed on the ball

return can sometimes halt a hard-hitting player in his tracks. The trick is to keep the ball much lower to the net than when defensive play was the dominating type of game. If you send your ball back too high, then the new bats will allow your opponent to kill you out of sight.

The loop was the killer stroke so far as the defensive craft was concerned. Some of the best players in the world were quickly put out of business, in particular Berczik of Hungary, now their extremely successful national coach. He had carried off three European titles with the heaviest backhand chop I've ever seen. But once the loop came in, he was forced to try and change his style and when he found he couldn't, had to retire. For a while, though, it did seem possible that some of the great defensive masters, such as Eberhardt Scholer of West Germany, would learn how to cope with it. Gradually, however, the sheer skill and cunning of the best attacking players, their different variations of topspin plus the new and increased speeds attained by using the reversed sandwich bats, made it more and more impossible for the purely defensive players to stay in the game.

Even the development of the anti-loop bat has not restored defensive supremacy. Its chief drawback is that, while it slows the game down and kills the loop, it does nothing at all for the man using it. He can only defend, never attack. Players such as Paul Pinkevich of Australia and Danny Seemiller of America use it to some extent on the rear side of their bats, reversing their grip suddenly so as to produce the unexpected dead shot. This has become its chief advantage.

Defence used to be played sideways on, but with the general speeding up of the game, most players now take a squarer stance to the table. I therefore advise a player on the forehand side to bend his body a little and put his head fairly near the bat. As for the bat itself, this ought to be in line with the striker's chin and the bat should be brought downwards and forwards in a simultaneous move. This will put the required backspin on the ball.

Incidentally, the quicker you bring your bat down, the more chop you give to the ball; the slower you bring it down, of course, the less chop.

One of the most commonly used strokes in the defensive game today is the topspin lob. You never use topspin unless you are attacking as a rule, but the lob is the one exception. In Richard Bergmann's day, the backspin chop was the great defensive shot, but no coach would allow a

Defensive chop

top player to use this today because it permits an opponent to use a loop against you. The topspin lob is very effective when your opponent is quicker than you and is forcing you away from the table by sheer pace. You play it very much like a normal forehand topspin except that you play it much further away from the table. I take the ball very low, reckoning that it will have lost much of its pace and spin by then.

The best way to make the shot is to bend your knees, take the ball low and loft it well over the net. Also hit it deep; if you try a short one your opponent will find it easy to kill. A deep ball not only puts your opponent under pressure but gives you time to get back to the table. Follow through, too. This will give the ball plenty of air crossing the net and make sure it falls deep into your opponent's half.

I suggest you practise the lob as much as possible. A good tip is to draw a line about six inches from the end of the table and try to lob every ball into those last few inches. This will also help to demonstrate how difficult it is for an opponent to get such a ball back. If you *face* a lob, on the other hand, return it down the backhand side of the table. This makes it difficult for your opponent to lob back and also reduces the chances that he will attempt to smash back at you.

Christian Martin finishing a defensive chop

There is another way to tackle a lob against you, but it's risky. This is to kill the ball quickly, taking it on the half-volley. You have to be very good to pull this one off.

The death of the backspin chop in defence and the arrival of the topspin lob is almost entirely due to the change in bats and the revolution in techniques that accompanied it. Today's bats are so fast that it's almost impossible to chop with them. The whole craft of the defensive is now moribund among men and, as I've said, to see the game played as it was twenty years or more ago, one has to study women's table tennis. From a spectator's point of view, this is much less rewarding. Compared with today's men's game, a match between women can too often seem pretty boring.

Another shot that is useful if you want to make your opponent overhit the table is the floater. You chop the ball but disguise your shot in such a way that your opponent cannot tell how much spin you have put on it. Invariably the spin gets him – he either overdrives or puts the ball so high that you can get in an easy smash.

The last part of your defensive repertoire – and however unfashionable the craft of defence might be I believe it is useful in breaking up the efforts of the whizz-kids who believe in nothing but attack – lies in your backhand. Play a backhand by starting with your bat at chin height, then bring it down and across the front of your body, the weight, so far as possible, on your back foot. The day of the long-range defence is over; or at least until somebody invents a new bat. But I still think the chop can be used to some advantage, particularly the backhand chop.

Some of the modern young players manage to mix the old and new in intriguing fashion. Pinkevich, for example, will counter-hit three or four times, everything on the half-volley, then suddenly put in a quick forehand or backhand chop. Against a player anxious to loop, or already looping, it's often good to get in and use a shorter stroke.

The chop is still a first-class stroke when you are up against penholders. Often it's a good idea to let them whack a couple of fast balls down at you, which you promptly whack back. Then you chop down their backhand and break-up their game by slowing them down.

Used properly, defence is actually a form of attack because it can slow down an aggressive opponent and allow you a chance to get back into the game.

DOUBLES PLAY○

DOUBLES○

The doubles game, of course, is as important in international team matches, as singles – although as in lawn tennis, it is the singles that gain most of the attention and glory. Most doubles players are, by nature, attacking players but it is advisable that one partner should be much steadier than the other. You need the steadier player to slow the attacking partner down a bit for if both attack all the time and happen to hit a bad spell, then the match will be over quickly and possibly a tournament will be lost.

It is always a good idea to match a more senior man with an eager youngster; he will keep the latter steady and give him the right encouragement if things start to go wrong.

There are two important points to remember in doubles: possibly the most important is that when you hit a ball, it is your partner who will have to deal with the return shot. The second is deciding the best order of play to follow – you'll often find that certain orders of play suit your partner better than you.

Normally the best doubles pairs are made up of a right-hander and a left-hander; this way both can get their forehand into action and also keep out of each other's way during the fastest moments of the game. However with really accomplished players, such as Jonyer and his compatriot, Gergely, world doubles champions in 1975 who can hit right or left, forehand or backhand and who can loop from either side of the table, such distinctions are superfluous. At anywhere but the supreme level, however, the basis of a good partnership is to be found in a good right-hander and a good left-hander playing alongside each other.

Usually, in today's table tennis, the shakehanders have an edge over the penholders. The Japanese game, based on the loop, provides a real threat but the Chinese because they stand close to the table, find

Danny and Ricky Seemiller of the U.S.A. in action

themselves getting in each other's way. When they step back a bit, they find the heavy loop kicking up too high for them.

The secret of good doubles play, once you have got the right mixture of partners, is to get together with your partner and study the play of your projected opponents. The trick here is to pick out which of them is the weaker of the two, and plan your campaign accordingly.

There are other important little points. Your partner should always have as good an idea as possible as to what kind of shot you intend playing. This is particularly true in the case of the service. A system of signals should be worked out between you, therefore. There's no point in putting in a quick serve or quick return if your own partner is as much taken by surprise as your opponents. When about to serve, therefore, you should clench your fist to show you're going to serve a fast one or perhaps hold out one finger to show you're going to serve a slow. It's important, of course, to make these signals under the table and out of sight of your opponent.

To play effective doubles, therefore, I advise as follows:

Attack in one corner. Dennis Neale and I always do this when we play doubles together. The advantage is that your opponents find themselves crowded and cramped and generally get in each other's way. Which is almost half the battle.

Doubles is an entirely different game to singles. Good singles players do not always make good doubles partners and vice versa. It is all a matter of bringing complementary talents and abilities into play.

Pick out the weaker opponent – if possible in your pre-match training. Then concentrate your play on him or her. You don't have to necessarily defeat the weaker player yourself; the idea should be to place your shot so that the stronger opponent is forced to return the ball in such a way that your partner can get in a winning stroke against the weaker player on the other side.

Always remember that when you've played a shot, get out of the way quickly.

Always remember that your partner has to take the return. This will often mean that you may have to sacrifice one of your favourite singles strokes – because the return wouldn't suit your partner. The test of a good doubles player is his ability to sacrifice his own favourite shots for the good of the partnership as a whole.

If you find your partner in brilliant form, don't start to compete with him. Let him go on winning the points as long as he can. Your job then is merely to keep the ball on the table and try and make openings for your partner when he is having a blue streak.

Always serve the ball as short as possible. This is intended to prevent your opponents from getting in a quick return at your partner before he can get set to take the shot.

Before beginning a game, talk over with your partner the shots he best likes to handle. In particular, discuss the service. There is no point in putting over a terrific spin service if your opponents are going to return it and leave your partner, who doesn't like dealing with heavy spin, in immediate difficulties. Particularly in the service, therefore, but indeed with every shot you make, try and remember that it is your partner who has to cope with the resulting difficulties.

MIXED DOUBLES○

It is very difficult to talk about the mixed doubles game at top level. The reason is that none of the really good men players will have anything to do with mixed doubles. I have said some unchivalrous things about women's table tennis but it is not that I mean to be unkind. One can only state the objective facts and when the top men have attempted to play mixed doubles, the games have become a farce. One shot – and the game is over.

For some reason, unlike lawn tennis where mixed doubles can be an enjoyable game to watch, mixed doubles in table tennis remains a very mediocre game. The primary reason, I think is the lack of option in table tennis. In lawn tennis, the partners can play as many strokes and in whatever sequence they choose. In table tennis, one player cannot hit two balls in succession, he must alternate with his partner. This means that the man is not able to take the weight of the opposing attack. His woman partner has to take the male serve or heavy return and at top level it has been found that even the best women players cannot survive long enough to make the game interesting. When a really world-class player sends over a loop, it can almost physically knock the woman over. Games have become farcical and mixed doubles has a very minor rôle in top table tennis.

Certainly, there is nothing in mixed doubles to interest the player who wishes to improve his game to the advanced levels. Therefore, if you do decide to take part in a mixed doubles game you have to work on two main assumptions: one, that the women are going to play what is essentially an old-fashioned defensive game; and two, that the concern you should always have for a partner in any doubles game needs to be very much greater in the case of mixed doubles. You must study the male partner in the opposing partnership and make sure that he gets a chance as rarely as possible to deliver a killer stroke at your partner. You must put him under such intensive pressure that the best he can do is to defend himself. If once allowed to get his attack going against your woman partner, you will quickly lose.

There are only a handful of women players who could hope to live for any length of time in fairly high men's company. Jill Hammersley of England, although her game is an anachronism compared with a man's, could give a good account of herself as could Alexandru of Roumania who chops the ball very heavily. In Rudnova, the Russians have a penholder of world class and Grimberg can deliver some tricky spin serves. Luzova of Czechoslovakia (now of West Germany) is a really fast counter-hitter, but the Chinese ladies, Lin Hui-Ching and Cheng Min-Chin are straightforward, although very correct, defensive players. Matsuzaki of Japan had a good, consistent topspin. Simon of West Germany is very useful with an extremely individual style: she chops and blocks close up to the table.

There are no real difficulties in the way of a good average woman club player improving her game provided she is prepared to practise with a man player of county level or above. But regrettably I cannot see any signs of real equality between men and women in table tennis in the foreseeable future. Until women are prepared to streamline their technique, the mixed doubles game will remain the Cinderella of table tennis matches.

THE BEST SHOTS PLAYED BY THE BEST PLAYERS.

The shot that has come to dominate modern table tennis at championship level is the loop and the players who have developed the technique for this demanding and sophisticated stroke inevitably lead the world. I. Jonyer of Hungary, the World Singles Champion in Calcutta in 1975 is a past master of both the forehand and backhand loop, but it is his backhand that his opponents find especially difficult to handle. Were it not that he suffers from temperamental weakness and can, too easily, be 'psyched' into defeat when up against tough opposition, his loops would make him a player who could rarely be overcome.

Another top class exponent of the shot is A. Stipancic of Yugoslavia. While Jonyer's especial skill lies in the backhand, Stipancic boasts a formidable forehand loop with vicious sidespin which can make the ball break either way. The unpredictability of this shot makes him particularly effective against the penholders who find that they are unable to read his intentions.

Other practitioners of the loop to be reckoned with include Gergely of Hungary who plays a strong modern attacking game, Secretin of France and Trevor Taylor, the British player who has joined the Dutch National team. His loop is strong on the backhand and forehand. Women players have not, on the whole, acquired the necessary skills for looping as their game is still based on defensive play. But one of the few women players who does use the loop is A. C. Hellman of Sweden who plays a strong counter-attacking game. However, she is weak on handling defensive play and thus is unable to exploit to the full her superiority with the loop. J. Magos Havas of Hungary is also an effective loop player.

The service can be a devastating weapon in the right hands and here some of the penholders come into their own. Men like Hsu Shao-Fa of

France's Jacques Secretin ending a forehand loop with a high follow through

China and his compatriot Hsi En-Tinh combine the ability to play brilliant angled shots with a wily and spinning service that often give them the advantage for the subsequent rally. Hsu Shao-Fa has perfected the art of difficult shots down to his opponent's backhand. Another Chinese with a good service and follow-up, this time a shakehand player, is Liang Ko-Liang. Although his game is fundamentally a defensive one, which makes it a little old fashioned by modern competitive standards, his serve and all-round skill keep him in the top class. He has made two changes in his game during his career, one successful change, one unsuccessful. The successful change was when he ceased to use the penhold grip and adopted the shakehand. The unsuccessful one was when in 1973 he tried to lose his defensive style of play and become an attacker, but never developed into a formidable one. A modern attacking player whose spin service is also a force to be reckoned with however, is Gergeley of Hungary.

The half-volleyers and counter-hitters are led by the Swede, Stellan Bengtsson, World Champion in 1973. This left-hander was sent to Japan to train six months before the World Championships, and the move paid off; indeed he led the European comeback that broke the Asian countries' growing superiority in the game. He likes to make his openings with his backhand shots forcing his opponents into error or vulnerability. His fellow Swede K. Johannson is an expert half-volleyer and counter-hitter as are M. Kohno of Japan and the young Desmond Douglas of Great Britain – like Bengtsson a left hander. Chen Min-Cheu, a penholder playing for the United States Team, is also noted for his counter-hitting prowess.

The forehand smash is another shot that brings out the best in K. Johannson who is perhaps the most gifted in this respect of those currently playing. His impeccable timing and exceptionally agile footwork give him an advantage over many an opponent, together with a dogged will to win and scrupulous fairness and chivalry during the match. Perhaps only Itoh, the Japanese ex-World Champion ever produced forehand smashes to rival Johannson, and Itoh was indeed legendary for his forehand. Charlie Wuvanich the United States player, formerly in the Australian team, is also renowned for his forehand smash but this penholder tends to lack consistency in his game and can be too erratic to keep up the pressure on his opponents.

The defensive game is still adopted by a number of top class players

Liang Ko-Liang of China executing a smash

even though it is less and less a match for the 'smash and grab' tactics of the best loopers. The penholder Lu Yuang-Sheng of China is a strong defensive player with great capacity for using spins. Secretin of France, an excellent all-rounder is strong in defensive play, as is the Hungarian Borzsei, who chops well against the loop. The latter uses a special anti-loop rubber on his backhand, a characteristic that he shares with the unorthodox Danny Seemiller of the U.S.A. Furukawa of Japan plays good defensive chops but lacks sufficient tightness in his game to take full advantage of this. The Australian Paul Pinkevitch reinforces his defensive game by having a racquet with different surfaces on either side which he turns constantly during rallies thus baffling opponents who cannot predict the speed of the return accurately.

Most of the women players still rely largely on the defensive mode of play. The exceptions – Hellman of Sweden, Magos Havas of Hungary and, to some extent, Jill Hammersley of Britain – have already been mentioned. Alexandru of Roumania is a shakehand player with a steady defensive game and will push and push the ball back over the net. Yet she lacks almost any techniques for attacking, and must therefore rely on wearing her opponents down. The Women's World Champion Pak Yung-Sun, a penholder from the Korean People's Democratic Republic, includes in her basically defensive game a great capacity for topspin while T. Ferdmann of Russia still a youngster, has potentially formidable skills with her half-volley and backhand. Another Russian, Rudnova, is a hard-hitter but subject to poor temperament and is too easily unsettled.

Of the players with a strong backhand Gomozkov of Russia has possibly the most penetrating of all world-class players, though his apparently lethargic approach to the game lets him down too often. Another Russian, Sarkhojan, is also noted for his backhand. Of the women T. Ferdmann, again of Russia, excels in backhand play.

But while many players may specialize in a particular shot, there are also those whose competitiveness depends upon their all-round competence and consistency. Men like Surbek of Yugoslavia may not be natural talents but nonetheless their persistence, will to win and physical fitness, together with hours of practice, have brought them to the top. Secretin of France is another man with all-round ability based on a defensive game, while the immense experience and consistency of Britain's Dennis Neale makes his game tactically formidable. Good temperament is also an important ingredient in success, and some of the most skilled players in the world such as Jonyer of Hungary and Stipancic of Yugoslavia may have more difficulty in winning the battle with themselves than with their opponent. As in all games the will to win and the refusal to be rattled by a run of failure or bad luck is often what brings an experienced and mentally well-integrated player out on top.

Charlie Wuvanich of the U.S.A. in action

Dennis Neale of England finishing a forehand

Danny Seemiller, U.S.A., performing his unorthodox backhand – really a forehand played in front of the body with the wrist turned over

Finally a word should be said about a few players who number un-orthodoxy amongst the weapons in their armoury. Sarkhojan deploys an unorthodox forehand in which he pulls the shot across his body. Not always effective, this may, however, baffle opponents by its unexpected peculiarity. Even more unorthodox is Danny Seemiller of the U.S.A. who uses a bat the reverse of which is covered in special anti-loop rubber. His extraordinary and highly effective backhand play is characterized by a technique of turning the wrists over so that the backhand is played from the forehand position. It looks extremely awkward but it succeeds in bewildering opponents by unpredictability of speeds and spins.

While players such as Seemiller and Sarkhojan are conspicuously un-orthodox it is also true that all the top players do what they do from in-stinct and individual preference built up from the long hours of grinding practice on the one hand, and individual characteristics of physique and temperament on the other. The great players in this as in other sports have an x-factor, which, when the chips are down, makes their game a winning one.

THE
NEW
PROFESSIONALISM○

The frontiers of the game are being continually pushed forward. Today the old nonchalant, play-it-for-fun days are over. Table tennis has become a matter of international prestige; it even plays a role in international diplomacy.

Almost as great a change has been the increasing professionalism inside the game. Much of this has resulted from the successes of the Far Eastern countries and the attitudes of the Iron Curtain bloc. There is no doubt that the Chinese lay great store by international success, although they sometimes appear to order their players to lose deliberately when playing nationals of a country with which they wish to establish good relations. Nor can there be any doubt but that the Iron Curtain countries see table tennis success as part of their psychological assault on the West aimed at convincing it of the superiority of their political system. I hasten to add, however, that whatever the political differences, the game is always played without rancour.

It was intensive coaching, dedication and practice that had much to do with Far Eastern successes in the 1950's. Sweden was the first European country to appreciate that the old amateurish methods were no longer good enough at international level and the first to appoint an international coach. The results they achieved were gratifying. They sent Bengtsson to Japan for six months before the world championships to train and acclimatise himself to Japanese methods, with the result that he brought back the world title to Europe. Thenceforward they approached the sport with the kind of seriousness shown by professional football clubs. Picked squads attended training centres every morning at 10 a.m., trained until midday, had a good luncheon, then resumed full--time circuit training and exercises in the afternoon. In addition their national squad was provided with an analysis of the styles and techniques of players from competing countries through lectures and films or video tapes.

This was merely copying the Chinese and Japanese regimes. The Chinese start their training day at seven a.m., run several miles before breakfast, practice with nets two feet high, strap sandbags to their legs and chop down trees to improve their muscles. Players are permitted little or no contact with the opposite sex during training. Such methods have now become fairly general among the leading table tennis countries. Some countries, however, spend more time, money and organisation on the sport with the result that their international successes are that much greater.

Sweden has become the great centre of organisation, dedication and professionalism in Europe (outside the Iron Curtain bloc). All moneys earned by the sport are ploughed back into it. Their top players are kept together *all the year round* and only leave their hotel or training centre at weekends to take part in big tournaments. Enormous attention and importance is given to ordinary club matches, seen as the backbone of the national effort. Most of the club teams are affiliated to important industrial firms and the players often work if only nominally, for these firms. The system, in effect, is modelled on that which has obtained in the U.S.A. for many years where universities have traditionally awarded scholarships or grants to good football players simply in order to produce a good university football team. Swedish firms, aware of the publicity value of a good club team affiliated to the firm, even import players from abroad, supply them with flats and houses and place them in lucrative jobs inside the firm. The system is paralleled behind the Iron Curtain where, as I said earlier, top players are often given lucrative state-subsidised jobs; there is the famous example of the stationmaster who has never seen the station he is supposed to run.

Throughout most of Europe, now, the approach to the game has begun to match that shown by the Swedes. In West Germany and in Holland, in particular, everything has become highly professionalised and the emphasis is increasingly placed on the money involved and the size of gates. Most of the best players belong to big clubs which are either affiliated to industrial firms, as in Sweden or, as is now becoming more fashionable, affiliated to famous football clubs, many of which run social clubs, where table tennis is an important activity. On the Continent, it is normal for a football club to be merely the centre of a variety of social activities. Increased size, and the connection with a famous football club, means that table tennis largely ceased to be an amateur pursuit, even at club level. Table tennis players are paid a salary in exactly the same way as football stars. Transfers are conducted along the lines of soccer transfers.

The game is not yet so professional in England, but is promising to become so. At the moment young Desmond Douglas has to work as a bus mechanic and if he takes time off for practice, loses money.

I am one of the lucky ones, but even I have to travel some two thousand miles a week, playing in tournaments, giving exhibitions, and lecturing, to do it. Potential world champions such as Trevor Taylor have been enticed away to Holland. Trevor now has a very well paid job there, a free house, and is allowed to keep any moneys he can earn on top of that through coaching, newspaper articles and lectures.

But I have no doubt that within the next few decades, even in England table tennis will become a worthwhile profession and capable of providing an entertaining and rewarding career for any youngster with talent. The place to begin is at school. Most of the leading table tennis countries now have a national schools' championship. If your school does not provide an opportunity, seek out a local club. In England, where the game is not so rigidly organised or encouraged as elsewhere, there are plenty of table tennis clubs. In London alone, there are no fewer than fifteen table tennis leagues. Each league has at least ten divisions, and there are at least fifteen clubs in each division.

In Sweden table tennis is now part of the general schools curriculum. I understand that similar developments are taking place in West Germany and Holland. In China promising young table tennis players are sent away to special schools where they study only a concentrated course on the game, a course sometimes lasting several years. The way to the top is the same in most of the leading countries. Start young, become prominent in your local school or local club team and if you show promise, ask to be put in touch with a good coach. In certain countries, all this is done for you. If you show promise at school or club level you will automatically draw the right attention and coaching will be provided.

At the age of seventeen a youngster should be ready to play in a county or state league, having graduated through local or district leagues and perhaps played also in inter-league tournaments. Once he arrives at county level, he is into the senior game. The best way to make progress thenceforward is to take part in as many open tournaments as possible. Many overseas countries grade their tournaments pretty strictly – that is, an entrant has to produce proof of his ranking. In such countries as England, however, most tournaments are open to all, and the best way to learn the game and study the new techniques is to play against better players.

Each country has its own national table tennis association which provides a list of tournaments which an aspirant can enter. The English Table Tennis Association is at 21 Claremont, Hastings, Sussex. The U.S. Table Tennis Association is at 1500 N. Broom Street, Wilmington, DE 19806. The magazine *Table Tennis* regularly publishes a list of all tournaments, at every level, throughout the world, together with information as to qualifications, entry forms and where to obtain them.

There is no simple avenue to success. To get ranked at national level and then eligible for selection to a national squad, a player must prove himself at the table. The only way to do this is to watch out for the important county or state championships; then go in for some of the closed championships before trying your luck in the opens. Once you have proved yourself in enough tournaments, you will earn yourself a place in the national rankings. Whether you can then make a career out of table tennis or not largely depends upon your personal skill and character. If you shine in world class circles, lucrative offers are soon likely to come your way.

APPENDIXES

RULES OF TABLE TENNIS ○

The Order of Play

In singles, the server shall first make a good service, the receiver shall then make a good return and thereafter server and receiver shall each alternately make a good return.

In doubles, the server shall first make a good service, the receiver shall then make a good return, the partner of the server shall then make a good return, the partner of the receiver shall then make a good return and thereafter each player alternately in that sequence shall make a good return.

A Good Service

The ball shall be placed on the palm of the free hand, which must be stationary, open and flat, with the fingers together and the thumb free. The free hand, while in contact with the ball in service shall at all times be above the level of the playing surface.

Serving shall then begin by the server projecting the ball by hand only, without imparting spin, near vertically upwards, so that the ball be visible at all times to the umpire and so that it visibly leave the palm.

As the ball is then descending from the height of its trajectory, it shall be struck so that it touch first the server's court and then, passing directly over or around the net, touch the receiver's court.

In doubles, the ball shall touch first the server's right half-court or the centre-line on his side of the net and then, passing over or around the net, touch the receiver's right half-court or the centre-line on his side of the net.

At the moment of the impact of the racket on the ball in service, the ball shall be behind the end-line of the server's court or an imaginary extension thereof.

Strict observance of the prescribed method of service may be waived where the umpire is notified, before play begins, that compliance is prevented by physical disability.

A Good Return

The ball having been served or returned in play shall be struck so that it pass directly over or around the net and touch directly the opponent's court, provided that if the ball, having been served or returned in play, return with its own impetus over or around the net it may be struck while still in play so that it touches directly the opponent's court. If the ball, in passing over or around the net, touch it or its supports it shall be considered to have passed directly.

In Play

The ball is in play from the moment at which it is projected from the hand in service until:

(*a*) it has touched one court twice consecutively;

(*b*) it has, except in service, touched each court alternately without having been struck with the racket intermediately;

(*c*) it has been struck by a player more than once consecutively;

(*d*) it has touched a player or anything he wears or carries;

(*e*) it has been volleyed;

(*f*) it has touched any object other than the net, supports, or those referred to above;

(*g*) it has, in a doubles service, touched the left half-court of the server or of the receiver;

(*h*) it has, in doubles, been touched by a player out of sequence, except as provided in law 15;

(*i*) it has, under the Expedite System, been returned by 13 successive good returns of the receiving player or pair.

A let

The rally is a let:

(*a*) if the ball served, in passing over the net, touch it or its supports, provided the service be otherwise good or be volleyed by the receiver;

(*b*) if a service be delivered when the receiver or his partner is not ready, provided always that a player may not be deemed to be unready if he or his partner attempt to strike at the ball;

(*c*) if, owing to an accident not within his control, a player fail to make a good service or a good return, or otherwise terminate the rally;

(*d*) if it be interrupted for correction of a mistake in playing order or ends;

(*e*) if it be interrupted for application of the Expedite System.

A Point

Except as provided in Law 9, a player shall lose a point:

(*a*) if he fail to make a good service;

(*b*) If, a good service or a good return having been made by his opponent, he fail to make a good return;

(*c*) if he, or his racket, or anything that he wears or carries, touch the net or its supports while the ball is in play;

(*d*) if he or his racket, or anything he wears or carries, move the playing surface while the ball is in play;

(*e*) if his free hand touch the playing surface while the ball is in play;

(*f*) if, before the ball in play shall have passed over the end lines or side lines not yet having touched the playing surface on his side of the net since being struck by his opponent, it come in contact with him or with anything he wears or carries;

(*g*) if he volley the ball;

(*h*) if, in doubles, he strike the ball out of proper sequence, except as provided in Law 15;

(*i*) if, under the Expedite System, his service and the 12 following strokes of the serving player or pair be returned by good returns of the receiving player or pair.

A Game

A game shall be won by the player or pair first scoring 21 points, unless both players or pairs shall have scored 20 points, when the winner of the game shall be the player or pair first scoring two points more than the opposing player or pair.

A Match

A match shall consist of one game, the best of three, or the best of five games. Play shall be continuous throughout, except that any player is entitled to claim a rest period of not more than five minutes duration between the third and fourth games of a match and of no more than one minute duration between any other successive games of a match.

The Choice of Ends and Service

The choice of ends and the right to serve or receive first in a match shall be decided by toss, provided that, if the winner of the toss choose the right to serve or receive first the loser shall have the choice of ends and vice versa, and provided that the winner of the toss may, if he prefers it, require the loser to make first choice.

In doubles, the pair who have the right to serve the first five services in any game shall decide which partner shall do so. In the first game of a match the opposing pair shall then decide similarly which shall be the first receiver. In subsequent games the serving pair shall choose their first server and the first receiver will then be established automatically to correspond with the first server as provided in Law 14.

The Change of Ends and Service

The player or pair who started at one end in a game shall start at the other in the immediately subsequent game and so on, until the end of the match. In the last possible game of the match the players or pairs shall change ends when first either player or pair reaches the score 10. In singles, after five points the receiver shall become the server and the server the receiver, and so on until the end of the game, except as provided below. In doubles, the first five services shall be delivered by the selected partner of the pair who have the right to do so and shall be received by the appropriate partner of the opposing pair. The second five services shall be delivered by the receiver of the first five services and received by the partner of the first server. The third five services shall be delivered by the partner of the first server and received by

the partner of the first receiver. The fourth five services shall be delivered by the partner of the first receiver and received by the first server. The fifth five services shall be delivered as the first five and so on, in sequence, until the end of the game except as provided below.

From the score 20-all, or if the game is being played under the Expedite System, the sequence of serving and receiving shall be the same but each player shall deliver only one service in turn until the end of the game. The player or pair who served first in a game shall receive first in the immediately subsequent game.

In the last possible game of a doubles match the receiving pair shall alter its order of receiving when first either pair reachers the score 10. In each game of a doubles match the initial order of receiving shall be opposite to that in the preceding game.

Out of Order of Ends, Serving or Receiving

If the players have not changed ends when ends should have been changed, they shall change ends as soon as the mistake is discovered, unless a game has been completed since the error, when the error shall be ignored. In any circumstances, all points scored before the discovery shall be reckoned.

If by mistake a player serve or receive out of his turn, play shall be interrupted as soon as the mistake is discovered and shall continue with that player serving or receiving who, according to the sequence established at the beginning of the match or at the score 10 if that sequence has been changed as provided in Law 14, should be server or receiver respectively at the score that has been reached. In any circumstances, all points scored before the discovery shall be reckoned.

Expedite System

If a game be unfinished 15 minutes after it has begun, the rest of that game and the remaining games of the match shall proceed under the Expedite System. Thereafter, each player shall serve one service in turn and, if the service and 12 following strokes of the serving player or pair be returned by good returns of the receiving player or pair, the server shall lose the point.

Definitions and Interpretations

(a) The period during which the ball is in play shall be termed a 'rally'. A rally the result of which is not scored shall be termed a 'let', and a rally the result of which is scored shall be termed a 'point'.

(b) The player who first strikes the ball during a rally shall be termed the 'server', and the player who next strikes the ball shall be termed the 'receiver'.

(c) The 'racket hand' is the hand carrying the racket, and the 'free hand' is the hand not carrying the racket.

(d) 'Struck' means 'hit with the racket, carried in the racket hand, or with the racket hand below the wrist'. A stroke made with the hand alone, after dropping the racket, or by the racket after it has slipped or been thrown from the hand, is 'not good'.

(e) If the ball in play comes into contact with the racket or the racket hand below the wrist, not yet having touched the playing surface on one side of the net since last being struck on the other side, it shall be said to have been 'volleyed'.

(f) The 'playing surface' shall be regarded as including the top edges of the table, and a ball in play which strikes these latter is, therefore, 'good' and still in play; if it strikes the side of the table-top below the edge it becomes out of play and counts against the last striker.

(g) 'Around the net' means under or around the projection of the net and its supports outside the table, but not between the end of the net and the post.

(h) If a player, in attempting to serve, misses the ball altogether he loses a point, because the ball is in play from the moment it is deliberately projected from the hand.

CHAMPIONSHIP TABLES ○

ENGLISH CLOSED CHAMPIONSHIPS

	Men's Singles	Women's Singles
1959-60	B. Merrett (Glos.)	Miss D. Rowe (Middx.)
1960-61	I. Harrison (Glos.)	Miss D. Rowe (Middx.)
1961-62	R.J. Stevens (Essex)	Miss D. Rowe (Middx.)
1962-63	C. Barnes (Essex)	Miss M. Shannon (Surrey)
1963-64	C. Barnes (Essex)	Miss D. Rowe (Middx.)
1964-65	C. Barnes (Essex)	Miss M. Shannon (Surrey)
1965-66	D. Neale (Yorks.)	Mrs. M. Wright (Surrey)
1966-67	I. Harrison (Glos.)	Mrs. M. Wright (Surrey)
1967-68	D. Neale (Yorks.)	Mrs. M. Wright (Surrey)
1968-69	D. Neale (Yorks.)	Miss J. Williams (Sussex)
1969-70	D. Neale (Yorks.)	Mrs. M. Wright (Surrey)
1970-71	C. Barnes (Essex)	Mrs. K. Mathews (Middx.)
1971-72	T. Taylor (Essex)	Mrs. K. Mathews (Middx.)
1972-73	T. Taylor (Herts.)	Mrs. J. Hammersley (Bucks.)
1973-74	C. Barnes (Essex)	Mrs. J. Hammersley (Bucks.)
1974-75	D. Neale (Yorks.)	Mrs. J. Hammersley (Bucks.)
1975-76	D. Douglas (Warwicks.)	Mrs. J. Hammersley (Bucks.)

	Men's Doubles	Women's Doubles
1959-60	J.A. Leach (Essex) and M.H. Thornhill (Middx.)	Miss D. Rowe (Middx.) and Miss J. Rook (Surrey)
1960-61	I. Harrison (Glos.) and B. Merrett (Glos.)	Mrs. E. Carrington (Essex) and Mrs. J. McCree (Essex)
1961-62	R.F. Raybould and R.J. Stevens (Essex)	Miss D. Rowe (Middx.) and Mrs. A.R. Mills (Middx.)
1962-63	R.F. Raybould and R.J. Stevens (Essex)	Miss D. Rowe (Middx.) and Miss M. Shannon (Surrey)
1963-64	D.O. Creamer (Middx.) and J.A. Leach (Essex)	Miss D. Rowe (Middx.) and Miss M. Shannon (Surrey)
1964-65	C. Barnes (Essex) and I. Harrison (Glos.)	Miss D. Rowe (Middx.) and Miss M. Shannon (Surrey)
1965-66	C. Barnes (Essex) and I. Harrison (Glos.)	Mrs. M. Wright (Surrey) and Miss K. Smith (Middx.)
1966-67	C. Barnes (Essex) and I. Harrison (Glos.)	Mrs. M. Wright (Surrey) and Miss K. Smith (Middx.)
1967-68	C. Barnes (Essex) and I. Harrison (Glos.)	Mrs. J. Billington (Essex) and Mrs. E. Carrington (Essex)
1968-69	D. Neale and A. Hydes (Yorks.)	Miss J. Heaps (Cheshire) and Mrs. P. Piddock (Kent)
1969-70	A. Hydes and D. Neale (Yorks.)	Mrs. K. Mathews (Middx.) and Mrs. M. Wright (Surrey)
1970-71	C. Barnes and T. Taylor (Essex)	Mrs. K. Mathews (Middx.) and Miss J. Shirley (Bucks.)
1971-72	A. Hydes and D. Neale (Yorks.)	Mrs. J. Hammersley (Bucks.) and Mrs. K. Mathews (Middx.)
1972-73	D. Neale (Yorks.) and T. Taylor (Herts.)	Miss L. Howard (Surrey) and Mrs. K. Mathews (Middx.)
1973-74	A. Hydes and D. Neale (Yorks.)	Miss L. Howard (Surrey) and Mrs. K. Mathews (Middx.)
1974-75	A. Barden (Middx.) and P. Day (Cambs.)	Miss C. Knight (Cleveland) and Mrs. K. Mathews (Middx.)
1975-76	D. Douglas (Warwicks.) and D. Neale (Cleveland)	Mrs. J. Hammersley (Bucks.) and Miss L. Howard (Surrey)

ENGLISH OPEN CHAMPIONSHIPS

Men's Singles	Women's Singles
1921-22	A. Donaldson (Durham)	Mrs. Scott (London)
1922-23	M. Cohen (London)	Miss K.M. Berry (Surrey)
1923-24	P. Bromfield (Kent)	Miss K.M. Berry (Surrey)
1924-25	P.N. Nanda (India)	Miss K.M. Berry (Surrey)
1925-26	R.G. Suppiah (India)	Miss G. Vasey (Whitby)
1926-27	R.G. Suppiah (India)	Miss D. Gubbins (Wales)
1927-28	Dr. D. Pecsi (Hungary)	Miss Erika Metzger (Germany)
1928-29	A Malecek (Czechoslovakia)	Miss M. Smidova (Czechoslovakia)
1929-30	S. Glancz (Hungary)	Miss D. Gubbins (Wales)
1930-31	M. Szabados (Hungary)	Miss V. Bromfield (London)
1931-32	M. Szabados (Hungary)	Mrs. M. Mednyanszky (Hungary)
1932-33	V. Barna (Hungary)	Miss D.M. Emdin (St. Albans)
1933-34	V. Barna (Hungary)	Miss M. Osborne (Birmingham)
1934-35	V. Barna (Hungary)	Miss M. Osborne (Birmingham)
1935-36	A. Ehrlich (Poland)	Miss M. Kettnerova (Czechoslovakia)
1936-37	V. Barna (Hungary)	Miss R. H. Aarons (U.S.A.)
1937-38	V. Barna (Hungary)	Miss D. Beregi (Hungary)
1938-39	R. Bergmann (London)	Miss J. Nicoll (Wembley)
1939-40	R. Bergmann (London)	Miss V. Dace (London)
1940/45	No contest	No contest
1945-46	B. Vana (Czechoslovakia)	Miss D. Beregi (Exeter)
1946-47	V. Tereba (Czechoslovakia)	Miss G. Farkas (Hungary)
1947-48	R. Bergmann (London)	Miss G. Farkas (Hungary)
1948-49	M. Reisman (U.S.A.)	Miss P. McLean (U.S.A.)
1949-50	R. Bergmann (London)	Miss M. Shahian (U.S.A.)
1950-51	A. Ehrlich (France)	Miss T. Pritzi (Austria)
1951-52	R. Bergmann (London)	Miss L. Wertl (Austria)
1952-53	M. Haguenauer (France)	Miss R. Rowe (Middlesex)
1953-54	R. Bergmann (London)	Miss L. Wertl (Austria)
1954-55	Z. Dolinar (Yugoslavia)	Miss R. Rowe (Middlesex)
1955-56	E. Gyetvai (Hungary)	Miss G. Farkas (Hungary)
1956-57	Z. Berczik (Hungary)	Miss F. Eguchi (Japan)
1957-58	F. Sido (Hungary)	Mrs. A. Simon (Netherlands)
1958-59	I. Ogimura (Japan)	Miss F. Eguchi (Japan)
1959-60	I. Harrison (England)	Mrs. A. Simon (Netherlands)
1960-61	V. Markovic (Yugoslavia)	Mrs. E. Foldi (Hungary)
1961-62	Z. Berczik (Hungary)	Miss D. Rowe (England)
1962-63	Z. Berczik (Hungary)	Mrs. M. Alexandru (Roumania)
1963-64	D. Giurgiuca (Roumania)	Mrs. M. Alexandru (Roumania)
1964-65	E. Scholer (W. Germany)	Miss M. Luzova (Czechoslovakia)
1965-66	European Championships held	
1966-67	J. Stanek (Czechoslovakia)	Mrs. M. Wright (England)
1967-68	S. Gomozkov (U.S.S.R.)	Miss E. Mihalca (Roumania)
1968-69	S. Gomozkov (U.S.S.R.)	Miss Z. Rudnova (U.S.S.R.)
1969-70	S. Kollarovits (Czechoslovakia)	Mrs. M. Alexandru (Roumania)
1970-71	T. Klampar (Hungary)	Mrs. M. Alexandru (Roumania)
1971-72	S. Bengtsson (Sweden)	Mrs. M. Alexandru (Roumania)
1972-73	S. Bengtsson (Sweden)	Mrs. B. Radberg (Sweden)
1973-74	K. Johansson (Sweden)	Mrs. M. Alexandru (Roumania)
1974-75	A. Strokatov (U.S.S.R.)	Miss E. Antonian (U.S.S.R.)
1975-76	S. Bengtsson (Sweden)	Mrs. J. Hammersley (England)

EUROPEAN CHAMPIONSHIPS

1958 Budapest, Hungary

MT	Hungary
WT	England
MS	Z. Berczik (Hungary)
WS	E. Koczian (Hungary)
MD	L. Stipec/L. Vyhnanovsky (C.S.S.R.)
WD	A. Roseanu/E. Zeller (Roumania)
XD	Z. Berczik/G. Lantos (Hungary)

1960 Zagreb, Yugoslavia

MT	Hungary
WT	Hungary
MS	Z. Berczik (Hungary)
WS	E. Koczian (Hungary)
MD	Z. Berczik/F. Sido (Hungary)
WD	A. Roseanu/M. Alexandru (Roumania)
XD	G. Corbizan/M. Alexandru (Roumania)

1962 Berlin, Federal Germany

MT	Yugoslavia
WT	Federal Germany
MS	H. Alser (Sweden)
WS	A. Simon (Germany FR)
MD	V. Markovic/J. Ieran (Yugoslavia)
WD	M. Shannon/D. Rowe (England)
XD	H. Alser/I. Harst (Sweden/GFR)

1964 Malmo, Sweden

MT	Sweden
WT	England
MS	K. Johansson (Sweden)
WS	E. Foldi (Hungary)
MD	J. Stanek/V. Miko (C.S.S.R.)
WD	M. Shannon/D. Rowe (England)
XD	P. Rosas/S. Lukacs (Hungary)

1966 London, England

MT	Sweden
WT	Hungary
MS	K. Johansson (Sweden)
WS	M. Alexandru (Roumania)
MD	H. Alser/K. Johansson (Sweden)
WD	E. Koczian/E. Jurik (Hungary)
XD	V. Miko/M. Luzova (C.S.S.R.)

1968 Lyon, France

MT	Sweden
WT	Federal Germany
MS	D. Surbek (Yugoslavia)
WS	I. Vostova (C.S.S.R.)
MD	A. Stipancic/E. Vecko (Yugoslavia)
WD	M. Luzova/J. Karlikova (C.S.S.R.)
XD	S. Gomozkov/Z. Rudnova (S.U.)

1970 Moscow, Soviet Union

MT	Sweden
WT	Soviet Union
MS	H. Alser (Sweden)
WS	Z. Rudnova (S.U.)
MD	D. Surbek/A. Stipancic (Yugoslavia)
WD	Z. Rudnova/S. Grinberg (S.U.)
XD	S. Gomozkov/Z. Rudnova (S.U.)

1972 Rotterdam, Netherlands

MT	Sweden
WT	Hungary
MS	S. Bengtsson (Sweden)
WS	Z. Rudnova (S.U.)
MD	I. Jonyer/P. Rosas (Hungary)
WD	J. Magos/H. Lotaller (Hungary)
XD	S. Gomozkov/Z. Rudnova (S.U.)

1974 Novi Sad, Yugoslavia

MT	Sweden
WT	Soviet Union
MS	M. Orlowski (C.S.S.R.)
WS	J. Magos (Hungary)
MD	I. Jonyer/T. Klampar (Hungary)
WD	J. Magos/H. Lottaler (Hungary)
XD	S. Gomozkov/Z. Rudnova (S.U.)

1976 Prague, Czechoslovakia

MT	Yugoslavia
WT	Soviet Union
MS	J. Secretin (France)
WS	J. Hammersley (England)
MD	S. Bengtsson/K. Johansson (Sweden)
WD	J. Hammersley/L. Howard (England)
XD	A. Stipancic/E. Palatinus (Yugoslavia)

U.S. NATIONAL CHAMPIONSHIPS

		Men's Singles	Women's Singles
1931	New York City	Marcus Schussheim (New York)	
1932	New York City	Coleman Clark (Chicago)	
1932	Newark	Marcus Schussheim (New York)	
1933	Chicago	James Jacobson (New York)	Jay Purves (Illinois)

Year	City	Men's Singles	Women's Singles
1933	New York City	Sidney Heitner (New York)	Fan Pockrose (New York)
1934	Cleveland	James McClure (Indiana)	Ruth Aarons (New York)
1934	New York City	Sol Schiff (New York)	Iris Little (New Jersey)
1935	Chicago	Abe Berenbaum (New York)	Ruth Aarons (New York)
1936	Philadelphia	Victor Barna (Hungary)	Ruth Aarons (New York)
1937	Newark	Laszlo Bellak (Hungary)	Ruth Aarons (New York)
1938	Philadelphia	Laszlo Bellak (Hungary)	Emily Fuller (Bethlehem)
1939	Toledo	James McClure (Indiana)	Emily Fuller (Bethlehem)
1940	Indianapolis	Louis Pagliaro (New York)	Sally Green (Indiana)
1941	New York City	Louis Pagliaro (New York)	Sally Green (Indiana)
1942	Detroit	Louis Pagliaro (New York)	Sally Green (Indiana)
1943	St. Louis	William Holzrichter (Chicago)	Sally Green (Indiana)
1944	St. Louis	John Somael (New York)	Sally Green (Indiana)
1945	Detroit	Richard Miles (New York)	Davida Hawthorne (New York)
1946	New York City	Richard Miles (New York)	Bernice Charney (New York)
1947	Chicago	Richard Miles (New York)	Leah Thall (Columbus)
1948	Columbus	Richard Miles (New York)	Peggy McLean (New York)
1949	New York City	Richard Miles (New York)	Leah Thall Neuberger (New York)
1950	St. Louis	Johnny Leach (England)	Reba Monness (New York)
1951	St. Louis	Richard Miles (New York)	Leah Thall Neuberger (New York)
1952	Cleveland	Louis Pagliaro (New York)	Leah Thall Neuberger (New York)
1953	Kansas City	Richard Miles (New York)	Leah Thall Neuberger (New York)
1954	Cleveland	Richard Miles (New York)	Mildred Shahian (Chicago)
1955	Rochester	Richard Miles (New York)	Leah Thall Neuberger (New York)
1956	White Plains	Erwin Klein (Los Angeles)	Leah Thall Neuberger (New York)
1957	South Bend	Bernard Bukiet (Cleveland)	Leah Thall Neuberger (New York)
1958	Asbury Park	Martin Reisman (New York)	Susie Hoshi (Los Angeles)
1959	Inglewood	Richard Gusikoff (New York)	Susie Hoshi (Los Angeles)
1960	District of Columbia	Martin Reisman (New York)	Sharon Acton (Los Angeles)
1961	Detroit	Erwin Klein (Los Angeles)	Leah Thall Neuberger (New York)
1962	New York City	Richard Miles (New York)	Mildred Shahian (Chicago)
1963	Detroit	Bernard Bukiet (New York)	Bernice Charney Chotras (New York)
1964	Inglewood	Erwin Klein (Los Angeles)	Valleri Bellini (Los Angeles)
1965	Detroit	Erwin Klein (Los Angeles)	Patty Martinez (San Diego)
1966	Detroit	Bernard Bukiet (New York)	Violetta Nesukaitis (Toronto)
1967	San Diego	Manji Fukushima (Japan)	Patty Martinez (San Diego)
1968	Detroit	Dal Joon Lee (Columbus)	Violetta Nesukaitls (Toronto)
1969	San Francisco	Dal Joon Lee (Columbus)	Patty Martinez (San Diego)
1970	Detroit	Dal Joon Lee (Columbus)	Violetta Nesukaitis (Toronto)
1971	Atlanta	Dal Joon Lee (Columbus)	Connie Sweeris (Grand Rapids)
1972	Hempstead	Dal Joon Lee (Columbus)	Wendy Hicks (Santa Barbara)
1973	Detroit	Dal Joon Lee (Columbus)	Violetta Nesukaitis (Toronto)
1974	Oklahoma	Kjell Johansson (Sweden)	Yukie Ohzeki (Japan)
1975	Houston	Kjell Johansson (Sweden)	Chung Hyun Sook (South Korea)
1976	Philadelphia	Dragutin Surbek (Yugoslavia)	Kim Soon Ok (South Korea)

WORLD INDIVIDUAL CHAMPIONSHIPS

	Men's Singles	Women's Singles	Men's Doubles	Women's Doubles
1926-27	R. Jacobi HN *bt Z. Mechlovits HN*	M. Mednyanszky HN *bt D.E. Gubbins WA*	R. Jacobi HN D. Pecsi HN	—
1927-28	Z. Mechlovits HN *bt L. Bellak HN*	M. Mednyanszky HN *bt E. Metzger GR*	A. Liebster AU R. Thum AU	F. Flamm AU M. Mednyanszky HN
1928-29	F.J. Perry EN *bt M. Szabados HN*	M. Mednyanszky HN *bt T. Wildam AU*	G.V. Barna HN M. Szabados HN	E. Metzger GR E. Rüster GR

1929-30	G.V. Barna HN *bt L. Bellak HN*	M. Mednyanszky HN *bt A. Sipos*	G.V. Barna HN M. Szabados HN	M. Mednyanszky HN A. Sipos HN
1930-31	M. Szabados HN *bt G.V. Barna HN*	M. Mednyanszky HN *bt E. Müller GR*	G.V. Barna HN M. Szabados HN	M. Mednyanszky HN A. Sipos HN
1931-32	G.V. Barna HN *bt M. Szabados HN*	A. Sipos HN *bt M. Mednyanszky HN*	G.V. Barna HN M. Szabados HN	M. Mednyanszky HN A. Sipos HN
1932-33	G.V. Barna HN *bt S. Kolar CZ*	A. Sipos HN *bt M. Mednyanszky HN*	G.V. Barna HN S. Glancz HN	M. Mednyanszky HN A. Sipos HN
1933-34	G.V. Barna HN *bt L. Bellak HN*	M. Kettnerová CZ *bt A. Krebsbach GR*	G.V. Barna HN M. Szabados HN	M. Mednyanszky HN A. Sipos HN
1934-35	G.V. Barna HN *bt M. Szabados HN*	M. Kettnerová CZ *bt M. Gal HN*	G.V. Barna HN M. Szabados HN	M. Mednyanszky HN A. Sipos HN
1935-36	S. Kolar CZ *bt A. Ehrlich PO*	R.H. Aarons US *bt A. Krebsbach GR*	R.G. Blattner US J.H. McClure US	M. Kettnerová CZ A. Smidova CZ
1936-37	R. Bergmann AU *bt A. Ehrlich PO*	*Title Vacant**	R.G. Blattner US J.H. McClure US	V. Depetrisová CZ V. Votrubcová CZ
1937-38	B. Vana CZ *bt R. Bergmann AU*	G. Pritzi AU *bt V. Depetrisová CZ*	J.H. McClure US S. Schiff US	V. Depetrisová CZ V. Votrubcová CZ
1938-39	R. Bergmann EN *bt A. Ehrlich PO*	V. Depetrisová CZ *bt G. Pritzi GR*	G.V. Barna EN R. Bergmann EN	H. Bussman GR G. Pritzi GR
1939-46	NO COMPETITIONS			
1946-47	B. Vana CZ *bt F. Sido HN*	G. Farkas HN *bt E. Blackbourn EN*	A. Slar CZ B. Vana CZ	G. Farkas HN G. Pritzi AU
1947-48	R. Bergmann EN *bt B. Vana CZ*	G. Farkas HN *bt V.S. Thomas EN*	L. Stipek CZ B. Vana CZ	M. Franks EN V.S. Thomas EN
1948-49	J. Leach EN *bt B. Vana CZ*	G. Farkas HN *bt K. Hruskova CZ*	I. Andreadis CZ F. Tokar CZ	H. Elliot SC G. Farkas HN
1949-50	R. Bergmann EN *bt F. Soos HN*	A. Rozeanu RU *bt G. Farkas HN*	F. Sido HN F. Soos HN	D. Beregi EN H. Elliot SC
1950-51	J. Leach EN *bt I. Andreadis CZ*	A. Rozeanu RU *bt G. Farkas HN*	I. Andreadis CZ B. Vana CZ	D. Rowe EN R. Rowe EN
1951-52	H. Satoh JA *bt J. Koczian HN*	A. Rozeanu RU *bt G. Farkas HN*	N. Fujii JA T. Hayashi JA	S. Narahara JA T. Nishimura JA
1952-53	F. Sido HN *bt I. Andreadis CZ*	A. Rozeanu RU *bt G. Farkas HN*	J. Koczian HN F. Sido HN	G. Farkas HN A. Rozeanu RU
1953-54	I. Ogimura JA *bt T. Flisberg SW*	A. Rozeanu RU *bt Y. Tanaka JA*	Z. Dolinar YU V. Harangozo YU	D. Rowe EN R. Rowe EN
1954-55	T. Tanaka JA *bt Z. Dolinar YU*	A. Rozeanu RU *bt L. Wertl AU*	I. Andreadis CZ L. Stipek CZ	A. Rozeanu RU E. Zeller RU
1955-56	I. Ogimura JA *bt T. Tanaka JA*	T. Okawa JA *bt K. Watanabe JA*	I. Ogimura JA Y. Tomita JA	A. Rozeanu RU E. Zeller RU
1956-57	T. Tanaka JA *bt I. Ogimura JA*	F. Eguchi JA *bt A. Haydon EN*	I. Andreadis CZ L. Stipek CZ	L. Mosoczy HN A. Simon HN
1958-59	Jung Kuo-tuan CH *bt F. Sido HN*	K. Matsuzaki JA *bt F. Eguchi JA*	T. Murakami JA I. Ogimura JA	T. Namba JA K. Yamaizumi JA
1960-61	Chuang Tse-tung CH *bt Li Fu-jung CH*	Chiu Chung-hui CH *bt E. Koczian HN*	N. Hoshino JA K. Kimura JA	M. Alexandru RU G. Pitica RU

1962-63	Chuang Tse-tung CH *bt Li Fu-jung CH*	K. Matsuzaki JA *bt M. Alexandru RU*	Chang Shih-lin CH Wang Chih-liang CH	K. Matsuzaki JA M. Seki JA
1964-65	Chuang Tse-tung CH *bt Li Fu-jung CH*	N. Fukazu JA *bt Lin Hui-ching CH*	Chuang Tse-tung CH Hsu Yin-sheng CH	Cheng Min-chih CH Lin Hui-ching CH
1966-67	N. Hasegawa JA *bt M. Kono JA*	S. Morisawa JA *bt N. Fukazu JA*	H. Alser SW K. Johansson SW	S. Hirota JA S. Morisawa JA
1968-69	S. Ito JA *bt E. Scholer GR*	T. Kowada JA *bt G. Geissler GD*	H. Alser SW K. Johansson SW	S. Grinberg SU Z. Rudnova SU
1970-71	S. Bengtsson SW *bt S. Ito JA*	Lin Hui-ching CH *bt Cheng Min-chih CH*	I. Jonyer HN T. Klampar HN	Cheng Min-chih CH Lin Hui-ching CH
1972-73	Hsi En-ting CH *bt K. Johansson SW*	Hu Yu-lan CH *bt A. Grofová CZ*	S. Bengtsson SW K. Johansson SW	M. Alexandru RU M. Hamada JA
1974-75	I. Jonyer HN *bt A. Stipancic YU*	Pak Yung Sun KD *bt Chang Li CH*	G. Gergely HN I. Jonyer HN	M. Alexandru RU S. Takahashi JA

AU Austria: CH China: CZ Czechoslovakia: EN England: GD German Democratic Republic: GR Germany: HN Hungary: JA Japan: KD Korea DPR: PO Poland: SC Scotland: SU USSR: SW Sweden: US United States: WA Wales: YU Yugoslavia.

* R.H. Aarons and G. Pritzi disqualified

WORLD MEN'S TEAM CHAMPIONSHIP—SWAYTHLING CUP

	No. of Teams	Winning Team	Team Members
1926-27	7	Hungary	B. Kehrling*, R. Jacobi, Z. Mechlovits, D. Pecsi.
1927-28	9	Hungary	Z. Mechlovits*, L. Bellak, S. Glancz, R. Jacobi, D. Pecsi.
1928-29	10	Hungary	Z. Mechlovits*, G.V. Barna, S. Glancz, I. Kelen, M. Szabados.
1929-30	10	Hungary	Z. Mechlovits†, G.V. Barna, L. Bellak, L. David, I. Kelen, M. Szabados.
1930-31	11	Hungary	Z. Mechlovits†, G.V. Barna, L. Bellak, L. David, I. Kelen, M. Szabados.
1931-32	10	Czechoslovakia	J. Kraus†, M. Grobauer, S. Kolar, J. Lauterbach, A. Malecek, F. Nickodem.
1932-33	11	Hungary	Z. Mechlovits†, G.V. Barna, I. Boros, L. David, S. Glancz, I. Kelen.
1933-34	12	Hungary	A. Wilcsek†, G.V. Barna, L. Bellak, L. David, T. Hazi, M. Szabados.
1934-35	17	Hungary	A. Wilcsek†, G.V. Barna, L. Bellak, T. Hazi, I. Kelen, M. Szabados.
1935-36	14	Austria	H. Nitschmann†, R. Bergmann, H. Goebel, H. Hartinger, E. Kohn, A. Liebster.
1936-37	13	U.S.A.	E.F. Cinnater†, A. Berenbaum, R.G. Blattner, J.H. McClure, S. Schiff.
1937-38	16	Hungary	A. Nattan†, G.V. Barna, L. Bellak, E. Foldi, T. Hazi, F. Soos.
1938-39	11	Czechoslovakia	R. Karlecek*, M. Hamr, V. Tereba, B. Vana.
1939-46	NO COMPETITION		
1946-47	18	Czechoslovakia	Z. Heydusek†, I. Andreadis, A. Slar, V. Tereba, F. Tokar, B. Vana.
1947-48	21	Czechoslovakia	V. Horvath†, I. Andreadis, M. Marinko, L. Stipek, F. Tokar, B. Vana.
1948-49	18	Hungary	G. Lakatos†, J. Koczian, F. Sido, F. Soos, L. Varkonyi.
1949-50	16	Czechoslovakia	A. Slar†, I. Andreadis, M. Marinko, V. Tereba, F. Tokar, B. Vana.
1950-51	24	Czechoslovakia	J. Hroch†, I. Andreadis, L. Stipek, V. Tereba, F. Tokar, B. Vana.
1951-52	15	Hungary	T. Bihari†, E. Gyetvai, J. Koczian, F. Sido, K. Szepesi, L. Varkonyi.
1952-53	14	England	A.A. Haydon*, R. Bergmann, B. Kennedy, J. Leach, A. Simons.
1953-54	33	Japan	K. Hasegawa†, K. Kawai, I. Ogimura, K. Tamasu, Y. Tomita.
1954-55	32	Japan	K. Hasegawa†, I. Ogimura, K. Tamasu, T. Tanaka, Y. Tomita.
1955-56	16	Japan	K. Hasegawa†, I. Ogimura, T. Tanaka, Y. Tomita, K. Tsunoda.
1956-57	33	Japan	C. Hodutsaka†, T. Miyata, I. Ogimura, T. Tanaka, K. Tsunoda.
1958-59	37	Japan	K. Hasegawa†, N. Hoshino, T. Murakami, I. Ogimura, S. Narita.
1960-61	26	China	Fu Chi-fang†, Chuang Tse-tung, Hsu Yin-sheng, Jung Kuo-tuan, Li Fu-jung, Wang Chuan-yao.
1962-63	45	China	Li Wen-yao†, Chang Shih-lin, Chuang Tse-tung, Hsu Yin-sheng, Li Fu-jung, Wang Chia-sheng.

1964-65	43	China	Fu Chi-fang†, Chang Shih-lin, Chuang Tse-tung, Chou Lan-sun, Hsu Yin-sheng, Li Fu-jung.
1966-67	41	Japan	K. Kimura*, N. Hasegawa, H. Kagimoto, S. Kawahara, M. Kono.
1968-69	46	Japan	S. Ohtsu†, N. Hasegawa, S. Inoue, S. Ito, K. Kasai, M. Kono.
1970-71	39	China	Hsu Yin-sheng†, Chuang Tse-tung, Hsi En-ting, Liang Ko-liang, Li Ching-kuang, Li Fu-jung.
1972-73	52	Sweden	C. Johansson†, S. Bengtsson, K. Johansson, B. Persson, I. Vikstrom.
1974-75	48	China	Ho Chu-pin†, Hsu Shao-fa, Liang Ko-liang, Li Chen-shih, Li Ching-kuang.
	* Captain		† Non-playing Captain

WORLD WOMEN'S TEAM CHAMPIONSHIP
MARCEL CORBILLON CUP

	No. of Teams	Winning Team	Team Members
1926-33	NO COMPETITION		
1933-34	6	Germany	H. Heim†, A. Felguth, A. Haensch, A. Krebsbach, E. Müller.
1934-35	11	Czechoslovakia	Z. Heydusek†, M. Kettnerová, G. Kleinová, M. Smidová.
1935-36	10	Czechoslovakia	V. Branny†, M. Kettnerová, G. Kleinová, M. Smidova, V. Votrubcová.
1936-37	9	U.S.A.	E.G. Cinnater†, R.H. Aarons, E. Fuller, D.P. Kuenz, J. Purves.
1937-38	10	Czechoslovakia	Z. Heydusek†, V. Depetrisová, J. Holoubková, M. Kettnerová, V. Votrubcová.
1938-39	5	Germany	P. Steffenhagen†, H. Bussman, G. Pritzi.
1939-46	NO COMPETITION		
1946-47	12	England	M. Knott*, E. Blackbourn, V.S. Dace, M. Franks.
1947-48	16	England	M. Knott†, D. Beregi, M. Franks, E. Steventon, V.S. Thomas.
1948-49	15	U.S.A.	J.H. McClure†, P. McLean, M. Shahian, T. Thall.
1949-50	10	Roumania	E. Horn†, A. Rozeanu, S. Slavescu, S. Szasz, E. Zeller.
1950-51	17	Roumania	E. Horn†, P. Patulea, A. Rozeanu, S. Szasz, E. Zeller.
1951-52	7	Japan	D.D. Daimon†, S. Narahara, T. Nishimura.
1952-53	10	Roumania	C. Comarnischi†, A. Rozeanu, S. Szasz, E. Zeller.
1953-54	23	Japan	Y. Tanaka*, F. Eguchi, H. Goto, K. Watanabe.
1954-55	22	Roumania	A. Gruia†, A. Rozeanu, S. Szasz, E. Zeller.
1955-56	8	Roumania	M. Vlaicu†, A. Rozeanu, E. Zeller.
1956-57	24	Japan	S. Minami†, F. Eguchi, T. Namba, T. Okawa, K. Watanabe.
1958-59	26	Japan	Y. Miyamoto†, F. Eguchi, K. Matsuzaki, T. Namba, K. Yamaizumi.
1960-61	19	Japan	K. Hasegawa†, T. Okada, K. Itoh, K. Matsuzaki, M. Seki.
1962-63	33	Japan	M. Miura†, K. Itoh, K. Matsuzaki, M. Seki, N. Yamanaka.
1964-65	31	China	Sun Mei-ying†, Cheng Min-chih, Liang Li-chen, Li Ho-nan, Lin Hui-ching.
1966-67	28	Japan	I. Ogimura†, N. Fukazu, S. Hirota, S. Morisawa, N. Yamanaka.
1968-69	37	U.S.S.R.	V. Ivanov †, L. Amelina, S. Grinberg, R. Pogosova, Z. Rudnova.
1970-71	27	Japan	H. Tanaka†, Y. Konno, T. Kowada, E. Ohba, Y. Ohzeki.
1972-73	40	Korea R.	Na In Sook†, Chung Hyun Sook, Kim Soon Ok, Lee Ailesa, Park Mi Ra.
1974-75	36	China	Lin Hui-ching†, Chang Li, Cheng Huai-ying, Hu Yu-lan, Ko Hsin-ai.
	* Captain		†Non-playing Captain

Former names of married women players:
Knott was Osborne
Müller was Rüster
Rozeanu was Adelstein
Szasz was Koloszvary
Thomas was Dace .